23487 4·00 *

HUMAN BODY

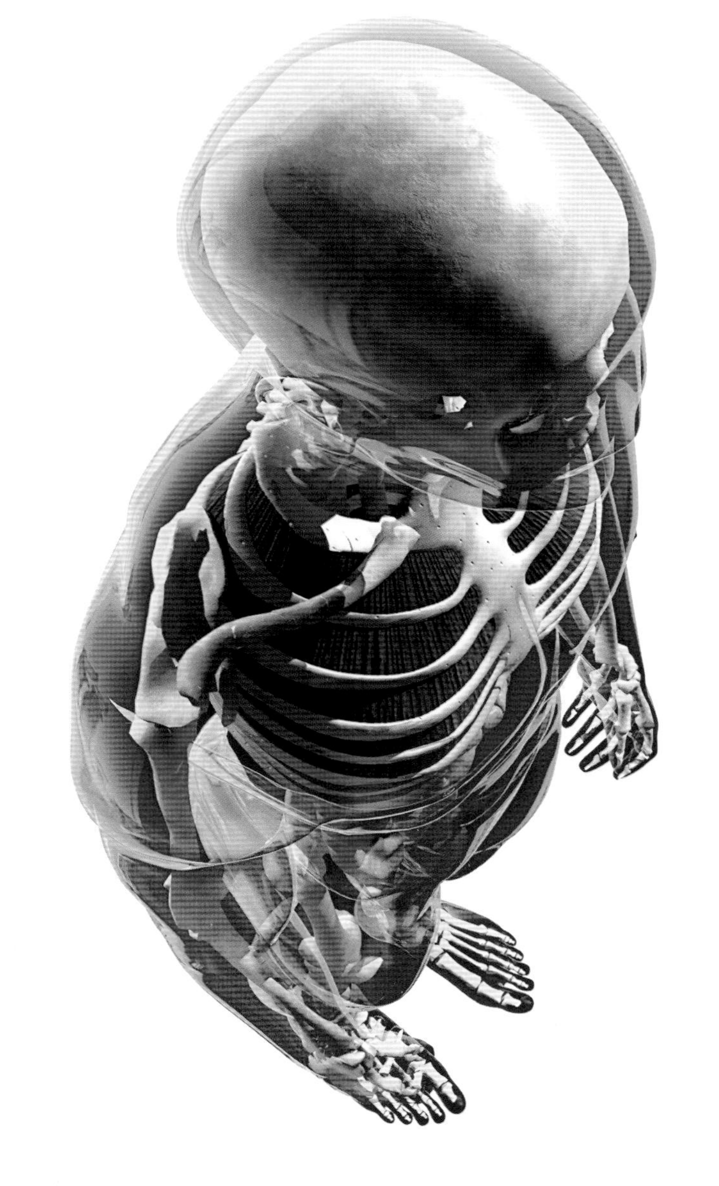

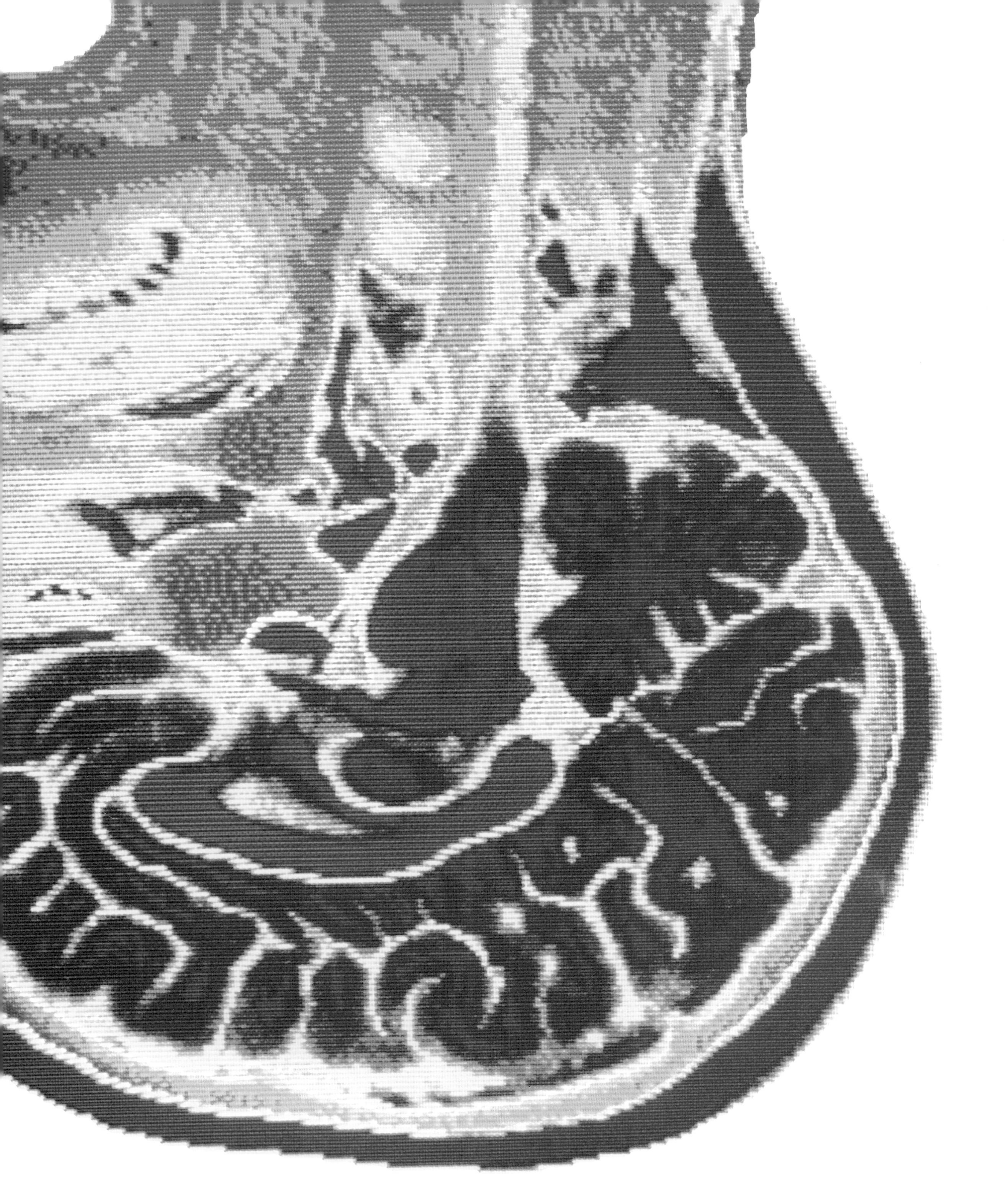

KINGFISHER KNOWLEDGE

HUMAN BODY

Richard Walker

Foreword by

Dame Professor Nancy Rothwell

KINGFISHER

Editor: Clive Wilson
Senior designer: Peter Clayman
Picture research manager: Cee Weston-Baker
Picture researcher: Rachael Swann
Senior production controller: Lindsey Scott
DTP manager: Nicky Studdart
Indexer: Sylvia Potter

GO FURTHER...
INFORMATION PANEL KEY:

websites and further reading

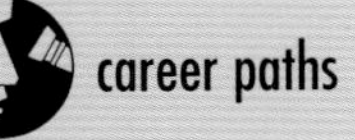
career paths

places to visit

KINGFISHER
Kingfisher Publications Plc, New Penderel House,
283–288 High Holborn, London WC1V 7HZ
www.kingfisherpub.com

First published by Kingfisher Publications Plc 2006
10 9 8 7 6 5 4 3 2 1
1TR/0506/TWP/MA(MA)/130ENSOMA/F

ISBN-10: 0-7534-1317-5
ISBN-13: 978-0-7534-1317-3

Copyright © Kingfisher Publications Plc 2006

All rights reserved. No part of this publication may be reproduced, stored in a retrieval system or transmitted by any means, electronic, mechanical, photocopying or otherwise, without the prior permission of the publisher.

A CIP catalogue record for this book is available from the British Library.

Printed in Singapore

NOTE TO READERS
The website addresses listed in this book are correct at the time of going to print. However, due to the ever-changing nature of the internet, website addresses and content can change. Websites can contain links that are unsuitable for children. The publisher cannot be held responsible for changes in website addresses or content, or for information obtained through third-party websites. We strongly advise that internet searches should be supervised by an adult.

Contents

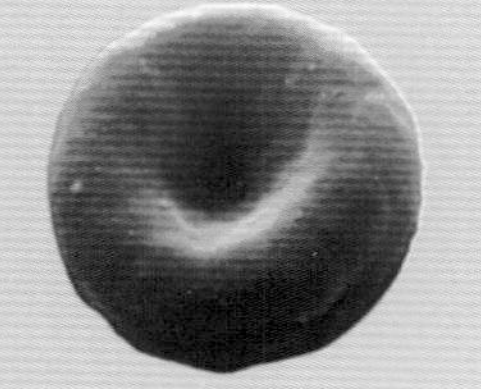

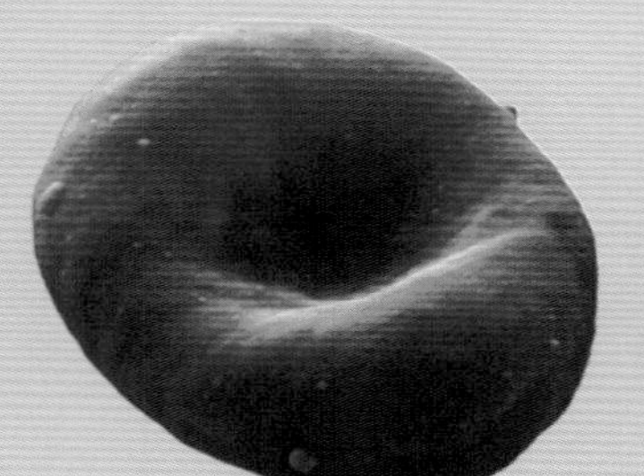

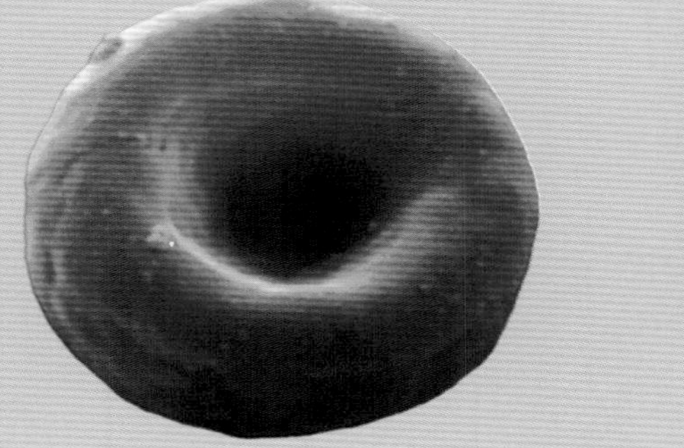

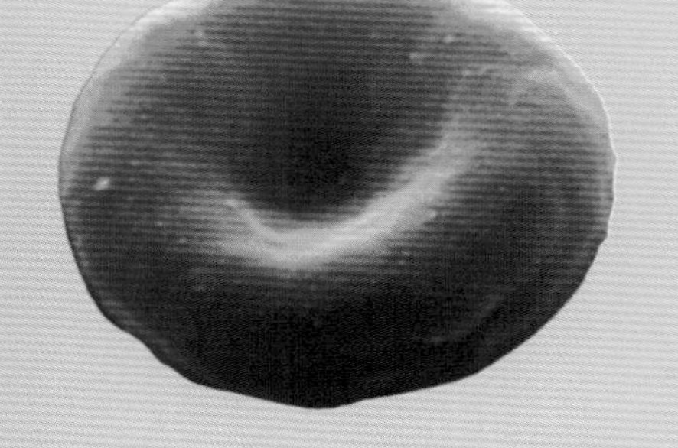

▶ This SEM shows red blood cells magnified nearly 2,500 times. One drop of blood contains more than 250 million red blood cells.

Foreword

The world we live in contains many fascinating and complicated things, but none as fascinating and complicated as ourselves. We may not be able to run as fast as a cheetah, smell our way home like a dog, catch prey like an eagle or dive like a dolphin, but as 'all-rounders' humans come out on top.

This book reveals fascinating facts about the human body and how it works. From the moment humans are born, tiny babies can control their breathing, their heart rate and how much blood is delivered to each part of their bodies. They can swallow, they know how much food they need and, within just a few days, they can begin to recognize people.

As we grow up we can adapt rapidly to cope with different surroundings or to face new challenges. For example, to keep cool in warm climates humans start to sweat more, or after exercise our hearts become more efficient.

At the turn of this century, scientists unravelled the code that controls the body's cells and how we are made. They worked out how to read these instructions, which are contained in DNA, and which make up the human genome. This turns out to be not so very different from other animals. But even small differences in genomes can have major consequences. Each one of us (apart from identical twins) has a slightly different genome. It is these differences that determine how tall we will grow, the colour of our eyes and, to some extent, our characters. But the human body is much more complicated than a set of genes. We are only just beginning to understand how our genes, and the world in which we grow up and live, influence the human body.

What makes humans really different to the rest of the animal kingdom is our brains. If you could peer inside someone's head, you would see the brain, the world's best computer. A collection of hundreds of millions of cells and millions of kilometres of connections allow us to think, remember and imagine. The brain also automatically controls almost every aspect of our bodies without us even knowing about it. My own research is trying to understand diseases of the brain and to develop new treatments to stop brain cells from dying when they are injured or do not get enough blood.

One day you too might become a scientist and help explore and unravel the body's intricate workings.

Professor Dame Nancy Rothwell, leading neuroscientist

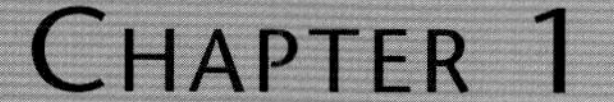

Chapter 1

Past and present

The fact that we can read the words on this page says a great deal about the human species, *Homo sapiens*. The ability to understand language is just one of the features that separate us from our fellow animals. Others include a large brain, a powerful intelligence and the capacity to solve complex problems.

An intense curiosity drove our human ancestors to explore the world, to develop civilizations and to express themselves through words, art and music. Over time they developed the technical and scientific skills that today allow us to understand how the body is formed and how it works. We have even learned how to read the instructions used to construct a human being.

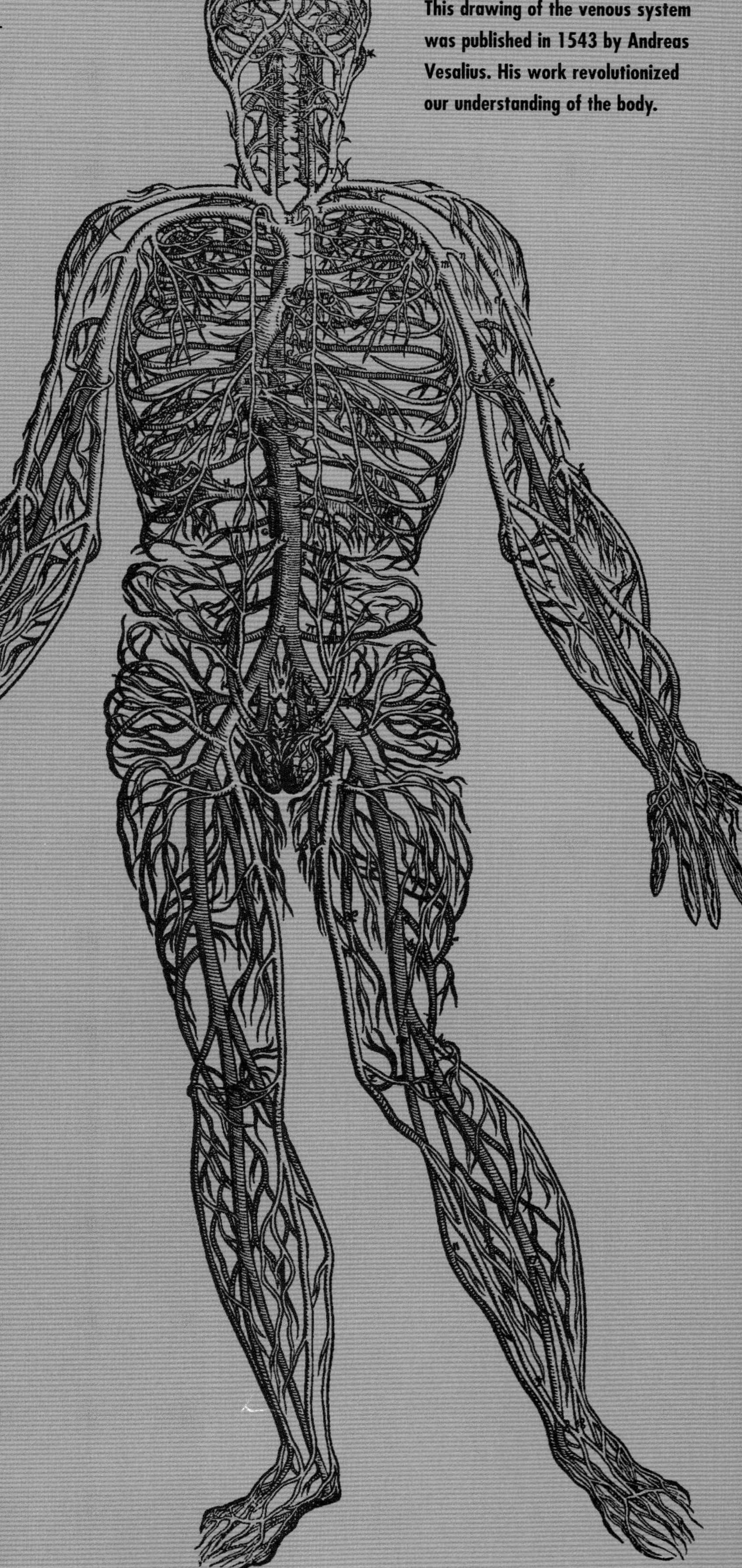

This drawing of the venous system was published in 1543 by Andreas Vesalius. His work revolutionized our understanding of the body.

Meet the ancestors

Our species (*Homo sapiens*) is the sole survivor of a many-branched family tree of humans. Early humans evolved from an ape-like ancestor that lived in Africa millions of years ago. Like gorillas and chimpanzees, human beings belong to a family of mammals called hominids. But humans stand out from other hominids because of their high intelligence, ability to use language, and technological and cultural advances.

◀ The bonobo, or pygmy chimpanzee (*Pan paniscus*), is our closest living hominid relative. Bonobos live in peaceful, female-dominated societies in the forests of central Africa. Their existence is threatened, however, by war and hunting.

Bony evidence

Evolution is the slow but gradual change in living things as certain individuals adapt better than others to changing circumstances. In time, this gives rise to new species. The story of human evolution has been pieced together by scientists called palaeoanthropologists. They study fossil bones and other remains to work out where and how early humans lived, and which ones were our direct ancestors.

▶ Humans are just as hairy as their ape relatives but their body hair is much shorter. Short hair meant that the first humans could sweat and lose heat more easily when they moved from cooler forests to hotter savanna millions of years ago.

▲ This chart shows the possible relationship of modern humans to some earlier hominin relatives. The family tree includes ancient hominid *Proconsul* (1), *Australopithecus* (2), *Homo erectus* (3), *Homo neanderthalensis* (4) and *Homo sapiens* (5).

The big split

The starting point for our story is between five and six million years ago with the big split in the hominid family. The first human (hominin) and the ancestor of today's chimpanzees and gorillas both arose from a common ape-like ancestor. Around this time, the climate in Africa cooled and became drier, while the forests shrank and were replaced by savanna – open plains with trees. Other hominids stayed in the forests, but the first humans emerged to face the challenge of savanna life.

Walking upright

What made early humans so different from their hominid cousins was their ability to walk on two legs – bipedalism. Walking this way uses far less energy, and allows the horizon to be scanned in search of food or enemies. It also frees up the hands for gathering food, for carrying objects and for making and using tools. Evidence for bipedalism comes from fossil footprints left 3.5 million years ago in Laetoli, Tanzania, by *Australopithecus afarensis*. This small-brained hominin may have been one of our ancestors. Later hominins included tool-user *Homo habilis* (2.3–1.6 million years ago), and fire-using *Homo erectus* (1.8 mya–100,000 years ago), which means 'upright human'. Scientists know from the size of its skull that *Homo erectus* had a bigger brain than its predecessors.

▲ A scientist holds the skull of *Homo floresiensis*. This hominin species – nicknamed the 'hobbit' because of its small size – was discovered in 2004 on the Indonesian island of Flores.

Out of Africa

Over millions of years of human evolution, the brain grew much larger. Increasingly intelligent hominins developed, while living and communicating in more complex social groups. The first modern humans appeared in east Africa between 150,000 and 200,000 years ago. These humans were the ancestors of all of us alive today. They could communicate using simple spoken language, and had a desire for problem-solving and exploration far greater than their ancestors. About 100,000 years ago *Homo sapiens* began its migration out of Africa. Within 80,000 years people had reached every part of the globe apart from Antarctica.

◀ A group of early humans gather at sunset. This is *Australopithecus afarensis*, a hominin up to 1.5m tall that lived between three and four million years ago in the savanna of east Africa. With only a chimp-sized brain, *Australopithecus afarensis* had limited intelligence but may have used simple tools such as sticks and stones.

Picturing the body

▲ Painted about 11,000 years ago, this rock painting from the Cave of the Arrows, Baja California, Mexico, shows men with upraised arms accompanied by various animals. The first cave paintings were made around 40,000 years ago, when there was a dramatic leap foward in the use of tools and communication.

We humans have a natural curiosity about the world around us, including how our bodies are built and how they work. Ancient paintings, made as long ago as 40,000 years, show human activity. From the time of the first civilizations, artists depicted the beauty of human form in paintings, drawings and sculpture. After the second century CE, understanding of the inner workings of the human body did not change much for well over 1,000 years. In the 1500s, however, a revolution in medicine occurred. From then until the present day, artists and anatomists – the investigators of human structure – have worked together to advance our knowledge of the body.

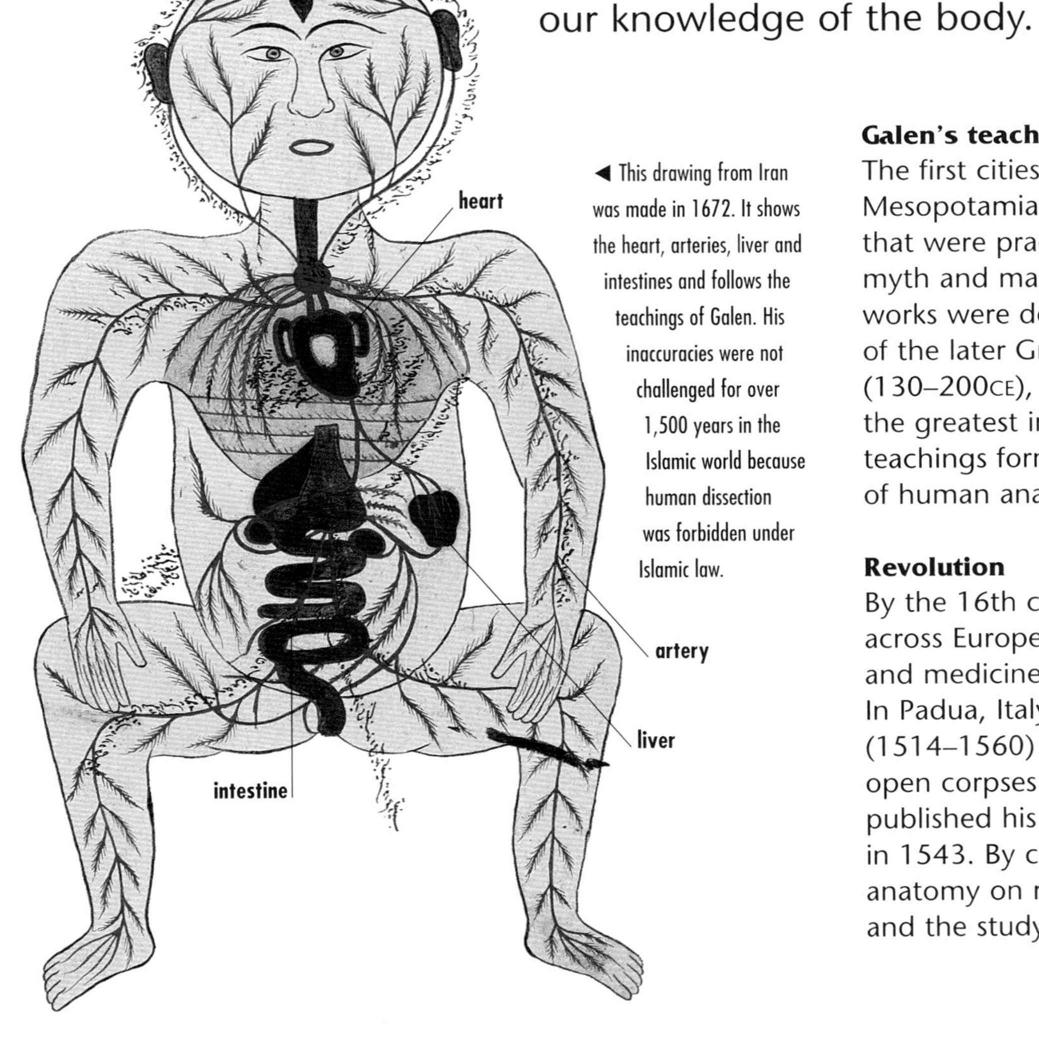

◀ This drawing from Iran was made in 1672. It shows the heart, arteries, liver and intestines and follows the teachings of Galen. His inaccuracies were not challenged for over 1,500 years in the Islamic world because human dissection was forbidden under Islamic law.

Galen's teachings

The first cities date from around 6,000 years ago in Mesopotamia (modern-day Iraq). The forms of medicine that were practised by these civilizations owed much to myth and magic. But some ideas about how the body works were developed by the great thinkers and doctors of the later Greek and Roman civilizations. Claudius Galen (130–200CE), a Greek doctor working in Rome, had the greatest influence. Although largely incorrect, his teachings formed the basis of people's understanding of human anatomy for the next 1,500 years.

Revolution

By the 16th century CE, the Renaissance was sweeping across Europe. This revolution in the arts, sciences and medicine challenged long-held ideas and beliefs. In Padua, Italy, the Flemish doctor Andreas Vesalius (1514–1560) carried out detailed dissections – cutting open corpses to investigate the body's structure. He published his anatomically correct illustrations (*see p.7*) in 1543. By challenging Galen's teachings, and basing anatomy on reality not myth, Vesalius allowed medicine and the study of the body to advance dramatically.

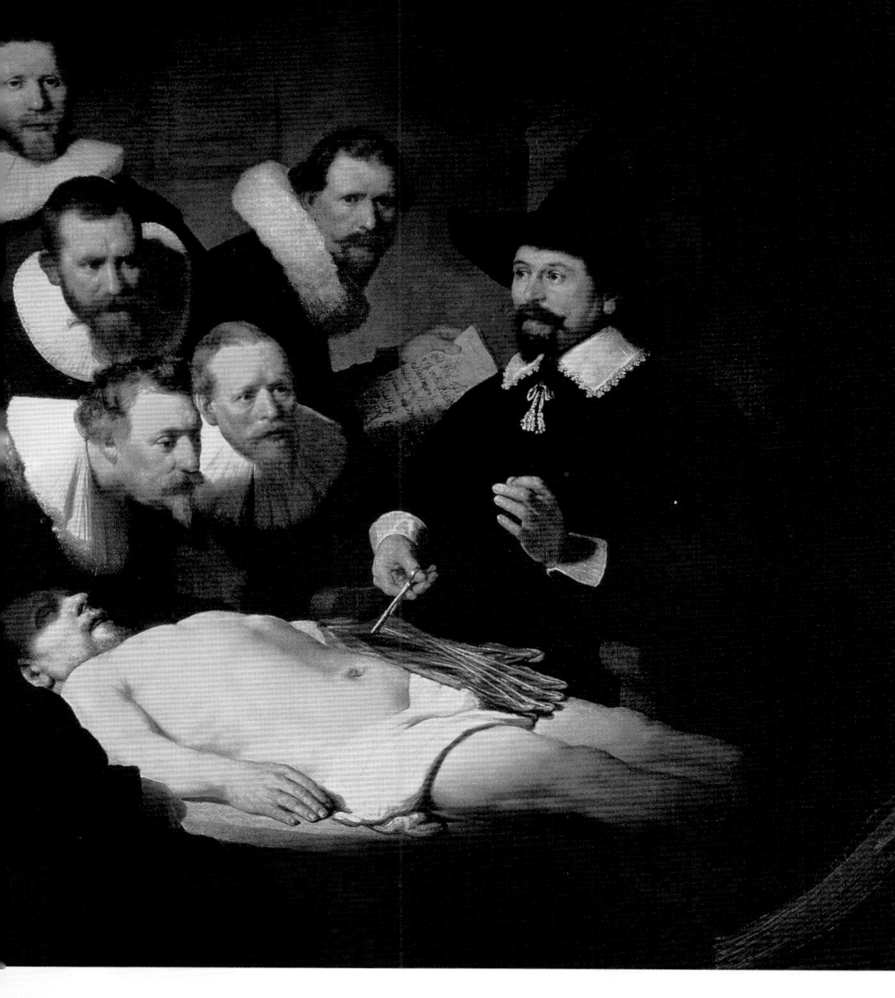

▲ *The Anatomy Lesson of Dr Nicolaes Tulp* was painted in 1632 by the Dutch painter Rembrandt van Rijn (1606–1669). In it, Dr Tulp (1593–1674) teaches the structure of the hand to seven fellow surgeons. The painting reflects the greater understanding of human anatomy, following the work of Vesalius.

Anatomy today

From the 17th century onwards, paintings, drawings, wax models and sculptures were used to illustrate and explain human anatomy. Today, artists still draw human dissections in order to make the anatomy as clear as possible. But now we have other ways of showing what lies under the skin. The Visible Human Project creates two- and three-dimensional images of the body that can be stored on computer. First, a dead body is cut into thin sections. Then, each section is photographed and the images used to create different views.

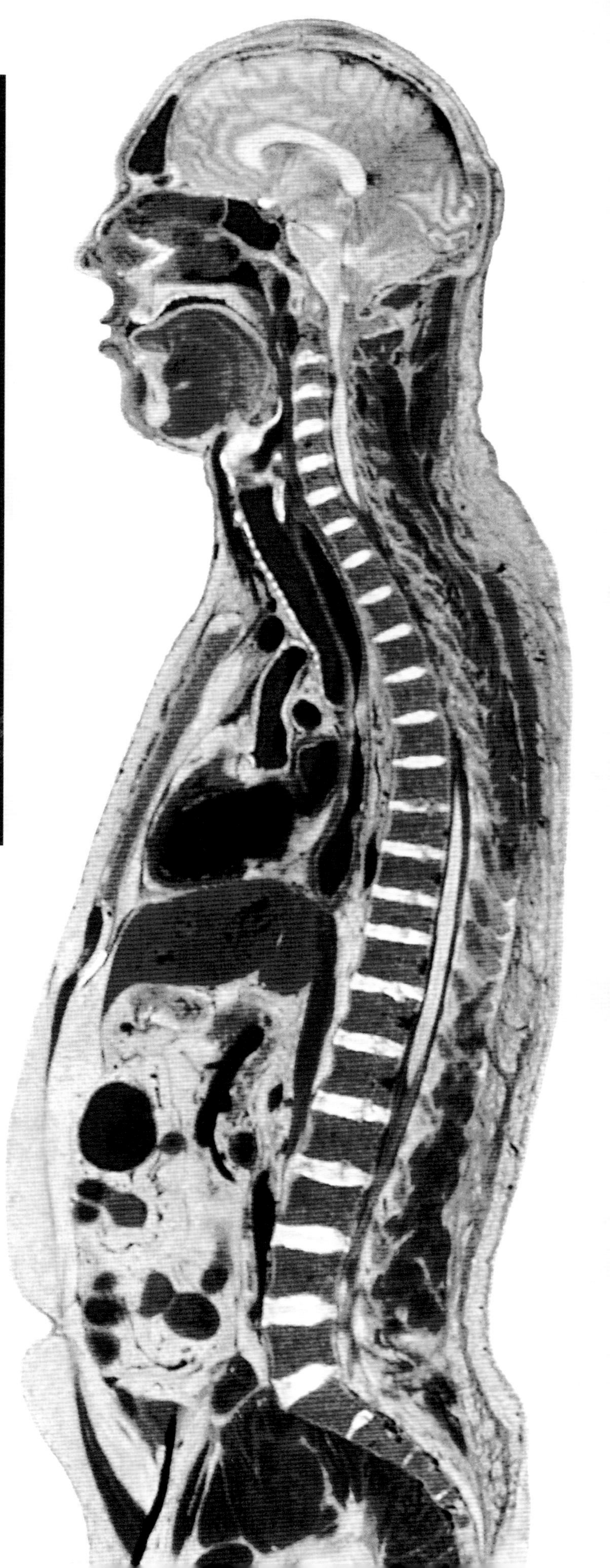

► This section of the male body is part of the Visible Human Project. It is produced using images from a sliced-up dead body and computer technology. The incredibly detailed results make it a very valuable research and teaching tool.

Living images

A range of technologies allows doctors and scientists to look inside a living human body without first having to cut it open. These techniques play a vital role in the detection of disease and investigating how the body works. Imaging techniques, such as X-rays, MRI scans and CT scans, create images of the body's internal parts. Viewing techniques, such as endoscopy, give a direct view of body tissues.

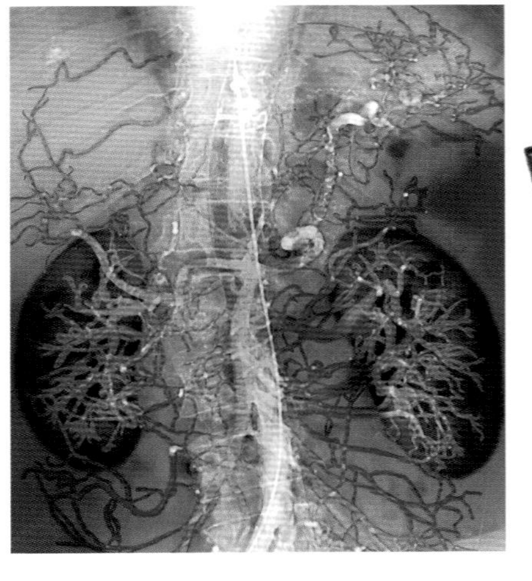

▲ In this X-ray, a special dye has been used to show up the arteries in the abdomen, including the aorta (coloured pink), which carries blood from the heart to other parts of the body. Two of its branches supply the kidneys (brown).

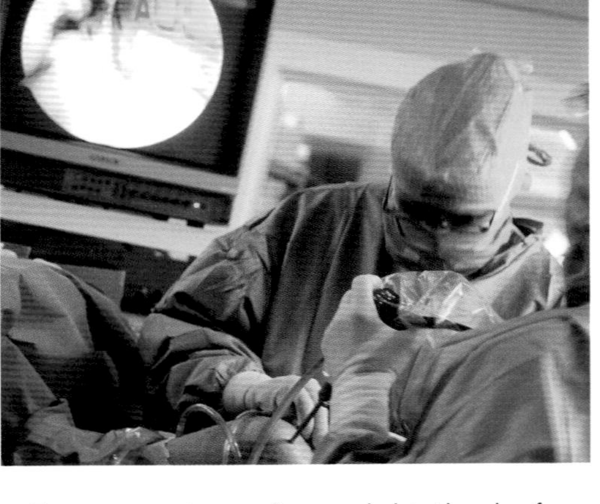

▲ This surgeon is using an endoscope to look inside and perform keyhole surgery on the patient's knee. On the screen is his view inside the knee joint. Keyhole surgery speeds up recovery time.

Through the endoscope

Endoscopy means 'looking inside'. It uses a tube-like instrument called an endoscope that is inserted into a natural opening, such as the mouth, or through a tiny opening made by a surgeon into a joint or cavity. Optical fibres inside the endoscope carry light into the body to illuminate the tissue or organ. The images are carried back along the fibres to an eyepiece or camera, so the doctor can see what is happening. Endoscopes allow doctors to perform keyhole surgery, in which surgical procedures are carried out through tiny incisions.

X-rays and CT scans

The first imaging method was developed in 1895 by German physicist Wilhelm Roentgen (1845–1923), who had just discovered a new type of radiation that he called X-rays. When, to his surprise, he passed X-rays through his wife's hand onto photographic film, an image of her bones appeared. X-rays were soon being used to detect bone fractures, as they are still today. Invented in 1972, CT (computed tomography) scanning combines X-rays and computers to produce images in the form of 'slices' through all types of tissues. These can be used to build up a three-dimensional image.

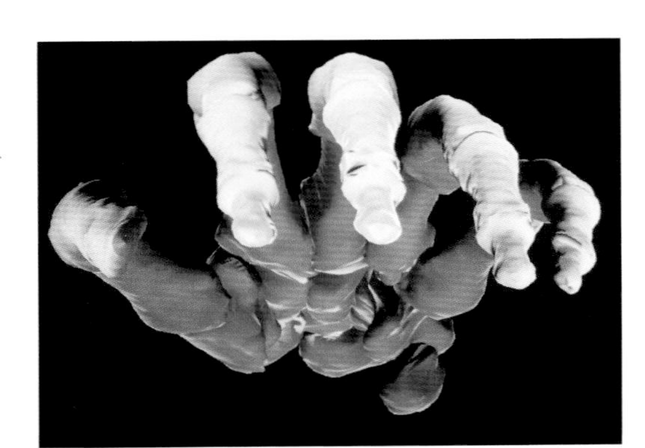

▲ This three-dimensional image of a living hand is produced by a CT scan, which sends beams of X-rays through the patient.

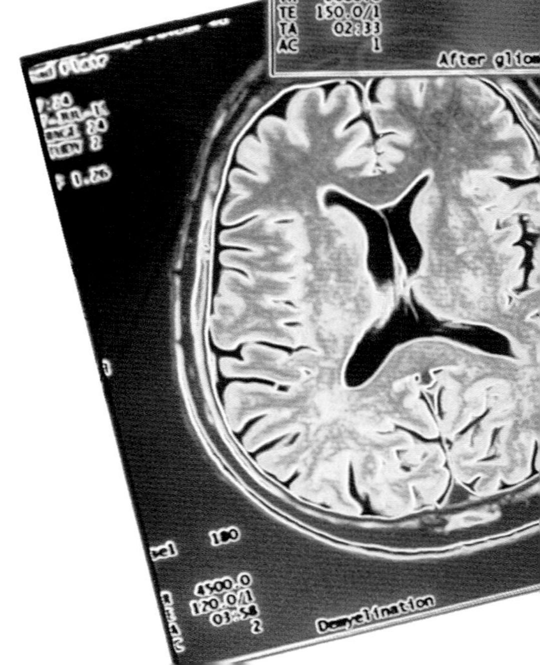

MRI scans

Magnetic resonance imaging (MRI) uses magnets and radio waves to produce detailed 'slices' through almost any part of the body. It is particularly effective for looking inside the brain, helping doctors to detect abnormal growths called tumours. The patient lies inside a tunnel-like scanner surrounded by a large, powerful magnet. Its magnetic field makes all the atoms inside the body line up. Then pulses of radio waves make the atoms fall out of line, and as they do so they send out tiny signals. These are picked up by a detector and turned into detailed images by a computer.

▲ A doctor examines MRI scans of a patient's head, selecting one that shows a horizontal 'slice' through the brain. His pointer highlights an unusual area at the rear of the brain which may indicate disease

Body ingredients

Our bodies are complex structures. So to understand how they are put together it is really helpful to think of them being organized as a sequence of levels – molecules, cells, tissues, organs and systems – that progressively get more complicated. Molecules are arranged in specific ways to form microscopic cells, the smallest parts of the body that are actually alive. Cells of similar types form tissues that provide the basic fabric of the body. Tissues are grouped together in organs that perform specific roles. Finally, linked organs fit together as systems.

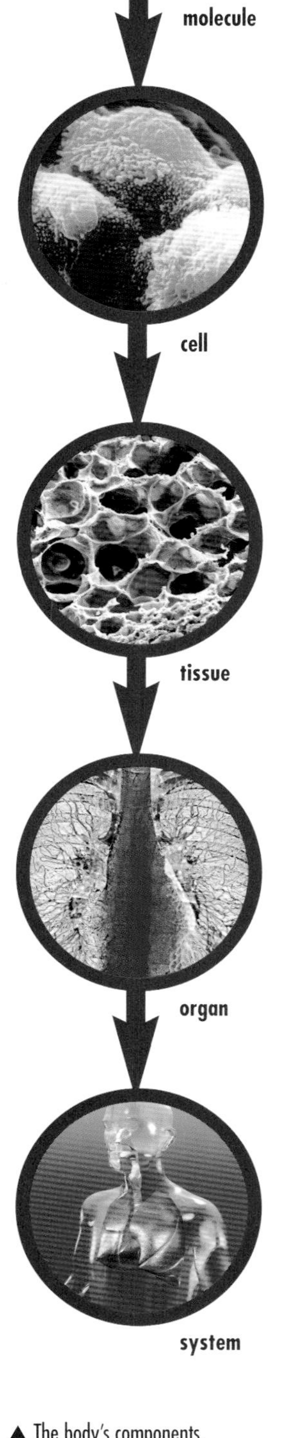

▲ The body's components, from the simplest to the most complex, work together to create a living, breathing human being.

▲ This computer model shows a molecule of glucose, a carbohydrate that provides the body's main energy supply. It consists of 24 atoms – six carbon (green), twelve hydrogen (white) and six oxygen (red).

Atoms and molecules

Thirteen key chemical elements provide our body's raw ingredients. The most common is oxygen, which forms about 65 per cent of body weight, mostly in the form of water. Others include carbon, hydrogen, nitrogen, calcium and iron. Other elements, including copper and zinc, occur in tiny amounts. Atoms of the commonest elements combine to form proteins, carbohydrates and lipids. These build cells or take part in chemical reactions known collectively as metabolism – the process that makes cells come to life.

Cells and tissues

The body's 100 trillion cells share the same basic structure and metabolism, but fall into 200 different types according to their shape, size and the job they do. Long nerve cells, for example, carry high-speed electrical messages, while plump adipose cells store fat. Similar cells that share a common function are grouped together in tissues, of which there are four basic types. Epithelial tissues cover the body's surface and line its cavities. Connective tissues bind, support and protect other tissues. Nervous tissues form the body's communication system. Muscle tissues move the body.

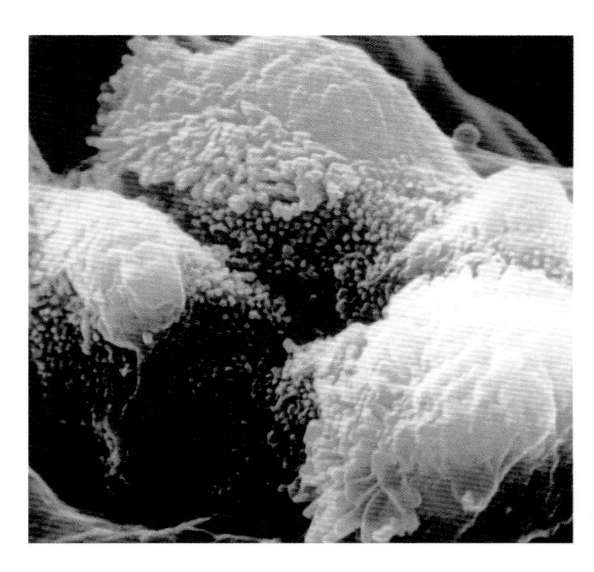

▲ In this SEM (scanning electron micrograph) are some of the cells – called epithelial cells – that line the millions of alveoli, or air sacs, found in each lung. Oxygen passes through the alveoli to enter the bloodstream.

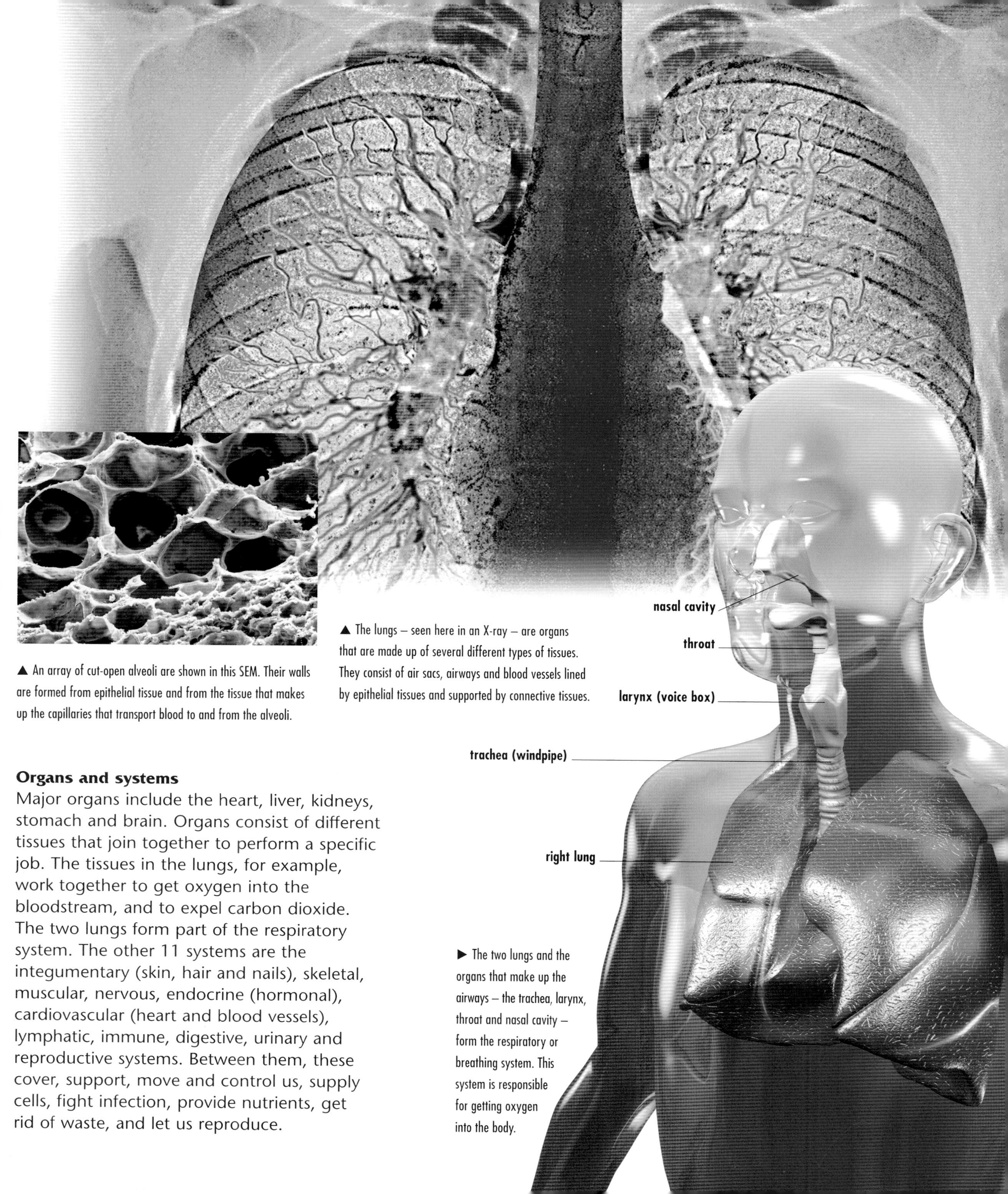

▲ An array of cut-open alveoli are shown in this SEM. Their walls are formed from epithelial tissue and from the tissue that makes up the capillaries that transport blood to and from the alveoli.

▲ The lungs – seen here in an X-ray – are organs that are made up of several different types of tissues. They consist of air sacs, airways and blood vessels lined by epithelial tissues and supported by connective tissues.

Organs and systems

Major organs include the heart, liver, kidneys, stomach and brain. Organs consist of different tissues that join together to perform a specific job. The tissues in the lungs, for example, work together to get oxygen into the bloodstream, and to expel carbon dioxide. The two lungs form part of the respiratory system. The other 11 systems are the integumentary (skin, hair and nails), skeletal, muscular, nervous, endocrine (hormonal), cardiovascular (heart and blood vessels), lymphatic, immune, digestive, urinary and reproductive systems. Between them, these cover, support, move and control us, supply cells, fight infection, provide nutrients, get rid of waste, and let us reproduce.

► The two lungs and the organs that make up the airways – the trachea, larynx, throat and nasal cavity – form the respiratory or breathing system. This system is responsible for getting oxygen into the body.

On the surface

Like a living overcoat, skin covers the body's surface to form a tough barrier between its delicate tissues and the outside world. Weighing up to 5kg, the skin is the body's heaviest and biggest organ. It has many functions, from filtering out harmful ultraviolet rays in sunlight to keeping our body temperature at around 37°C. The skin is also waterproof, germ-proof, self-repairing and houses sensors that allow us to feel touch, pressure, heat, cold and pain.

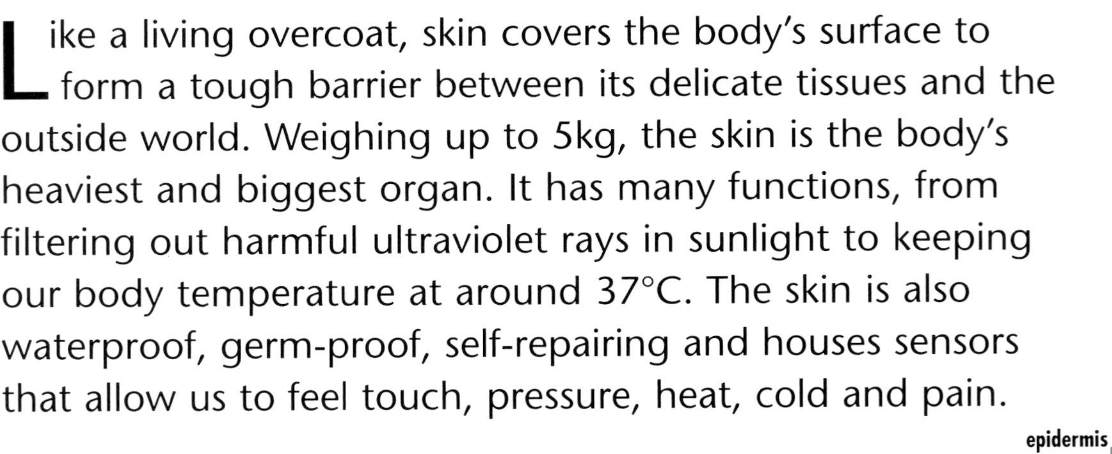

▲ Ridges and grooves are found on the skin covering the undersides of the hands and feet. They form curved patterns unique to each individual. The tiny dents along the ridges are the openings of sweat glands from which sweat pours onto the skin's surface.

Surface features

While our skin's surface may appear smooth, it is in fact covered in bumps, ridges and grooves in which billions of bacteria lurk. The openings of sweat glands and hair follicles, from which hair grows, are also found here. Skin is kept soft and supple by oily sebum released from glands deeper in the skin. The ridges and grooves on the underside of our fingers help us to grip and leave behind greasy, sweaty marks known as fingerprints.

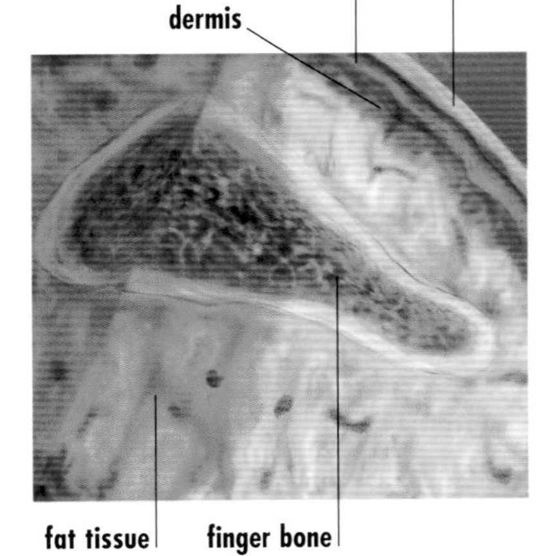

▶ This cross-section of a fingertip shows a slice through a nail, skin, fat and bone. Under the nail, the skin's two layers – the epidermis and dermis – can be clearly seen.

Hair and nails

Hairs are long, flexible strands of tough, dead cells that grow from pits in the skin called hair follicles. Living cells at the base of a hair divide to push the hair shaft above the skin's surface. Long hairs grow from the scalp, protecting it and helping to keep the head warm. Shorter, finer hairs on the rest of the body make our skin more sensitive to touch. Nails grow from living cells in the nail's root.

▼ Skin and hair colour ranges from fair to dark. Their colour is determined by the amount of a brown colouring called melanin. Hair can be straight, curly or wavy and depends on the shape of the hair follicles in the skin.

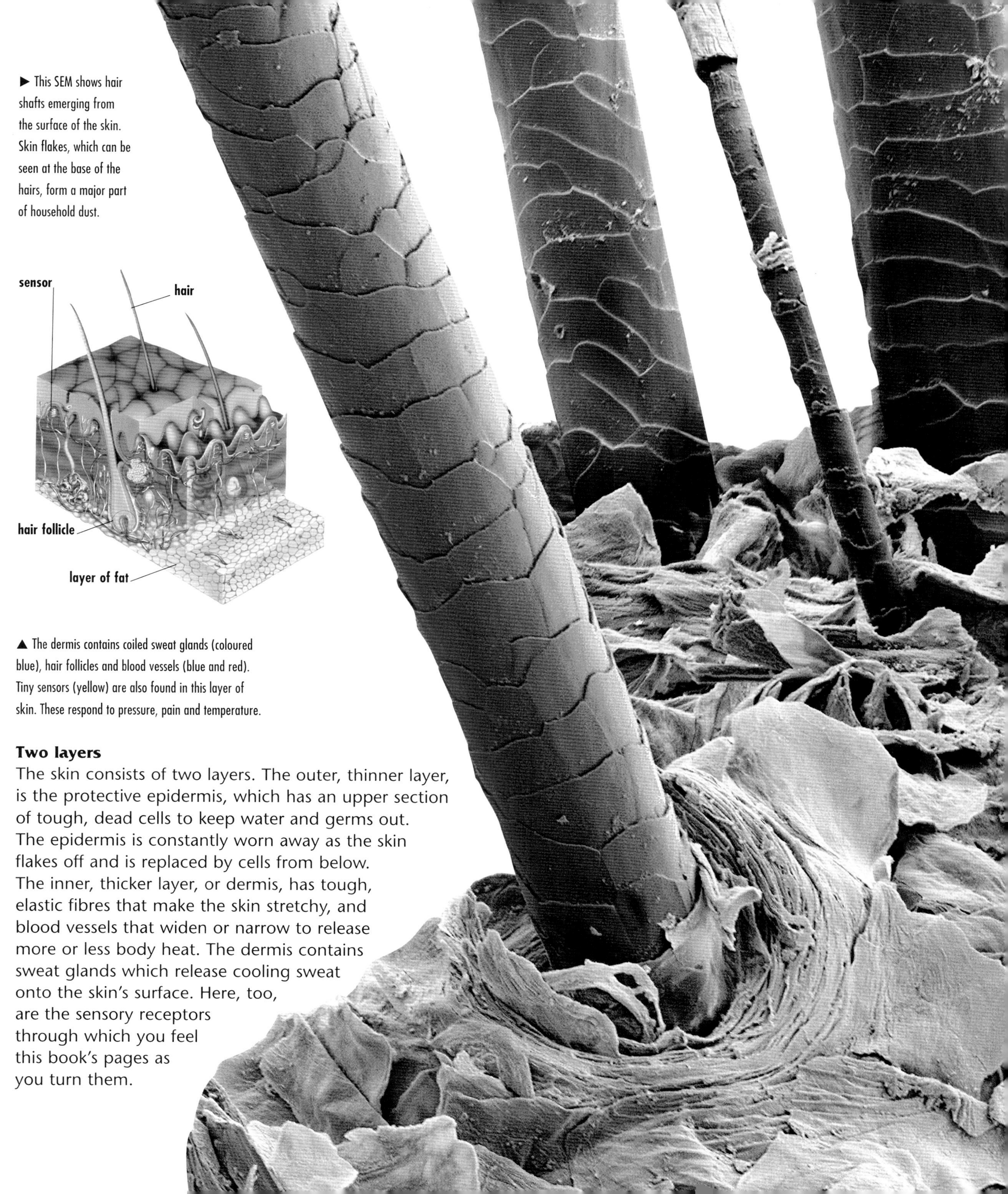

▶ This SEM shows hair shafts emerging from the surface of the skin. Skin flakes, which can be seen at the base of the hairs, form a major part of household dust.

▲ The dermis contains coiled sweat glands (coloured blue), hair follicles and blood vessels (blue and red). Tiny sensors (yellow) are also found in this layer of skin. These respond to pressure, pain and temperature.

Two layers

The skin consists of two layers. The outer, thinner layer, is the protective epidermis, which has an upper section of tough, dead cells to keep water and germs out. The epidermis is constantly worn away as the skin flakes off and is replaced by cells from below. The inner, thicker layer, or dermis, has tough, elastic fibres that make the skin stretchy, and blood vessels that widen or narrow to release more or less body heat. The dermis contains sweat glands which release cooling sweat onto the skin's surface. Here, too, are the sensory receptors through which you feel this book's pages as you turn them.

◀ A scientist holds an autoradiogram. This photographic record shows the banding pattern produced when DNA is cut up into fragments and separated. We share a remarkable 99.9 per cent of our DNA with other humans. It is that 0.1 per cent difference that makes us individuals.

Instructions for life

From germ-battling white blood cells to information-processing brain cells, all of our body cells contain the instructions needed to build and run a human being. Those instructions are held inside each cell's nucleus on long, thread-like structures called chromosomes. The chromosomes are made from a chemical called DNA (deoxyribonucleic acid). DNA is divided into sections called genes, each of which is a coded instruction. When we reproduce, we pass on genes to our offspring.

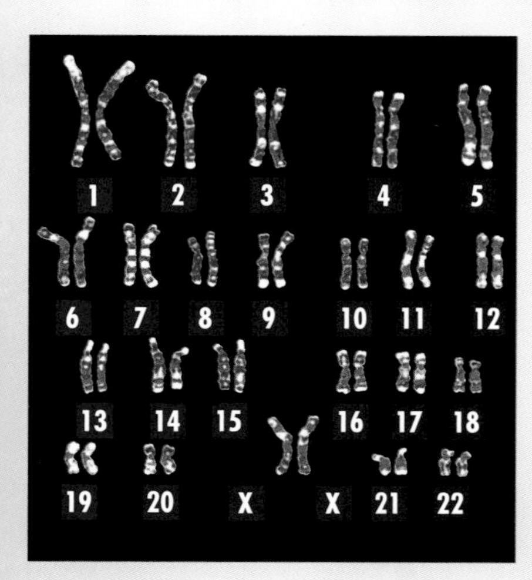

◀ This karyotype shows a complete set of chromosomes from a female. It is prepared by photographing chromosomes, then arranging chromosome pairs in size order from biggest (pair 1) to smallest (pair 22). The female sex chromosomes (XX) are centre bottom. In males (XY), the Y chromosome is much smaller than the X.

Chromosomes and genes

Look inside the nucleus of most body cells and you will find 46 chromosomes. Or, put another way, there are two sets of 23 paired chromosomes, one set inherited from our mother and one from our father. Each set of chromosomes contains a full set of human-building genes and is called a genome. In 2003 the Human Genome Project (HGP) analyzed the DNA in human cells as a first step to identifying all our genes and what they do. Scientists working on the HGP discovered that each genome contains about 25,000 genes.

DNA base

▼ This computer image shows a human chromosome in its characteristic X-shape. The coloured bands, which mark the position of the genes, are created by staining the chromosome. Each type of chromosome has a unique banding pattern.

DNA at work

Each DNA molecule consists of two long strands twisted together to form a spiralling double helix. Each strand is made up of a sequence of four 'bases' called adenine (A), cytosine (C), guanine (G) and thymine (T). The specific sequence of bases – A, C, G and T – in each gene forms the letters of a coded message. This tells the cell how to make just one of the thousands of different types of proteins that are involved in building a human body.

Family tree

Can you roll your tongue or are your eyes brown or blue? These are just two of the body features controlled by the genes inherited from our parents. Most of the paired genes on our two sets of chromosomes are identical. But some occur as alleles – slightly different versions of the same gene. And while one allele makes proteins, its opposite number stays 'switched off'. This explains why we resemble our parents but are not exact copies.

▼ In three generations of the same family, each individual has a unique set of genes. However, because most of the genes are identical to the earlier generation, clear family resemblances are visible.

▼ There are 46 chromosomes found in the nucleus of each cell. Each chromosome is made up of a DNA double helix that is very tightly coiled up. Unravelled, as shown here, a chromosome resembles a spiralling ladder.

Making babies

Like all other living organisms, humans reproduce to make the babies that will eventually replace their parents as they age and die. Reproduction is carried out by the reproductive system, the only body system to differ significantly between the sexes. Both systems 'switch on' at puberty. The female system releases sex cells called eggs, or ova, while the male system makes sex cells called sperm. When these sex cells join together, their combined DNA contains all the information needed to construct a new human being.

▼ This SEM captures the moment of ovulation. An egg (coloured pink) surrounded by follicle cells (white) has burst out from its swollen follicle, lying just below the surface of the ovary (orange). Hundreds of thousands of immature eggs are already present inside the two ovaries before a girl is born.

▶ The main components of the female reproductive system, shown here in front view, include the two ovaries and, in cross-section, the fallopian tubes, uterus and vagina. As well as making sex cells, the female system also provides the location where egg and sperm meet, and a baby develops.

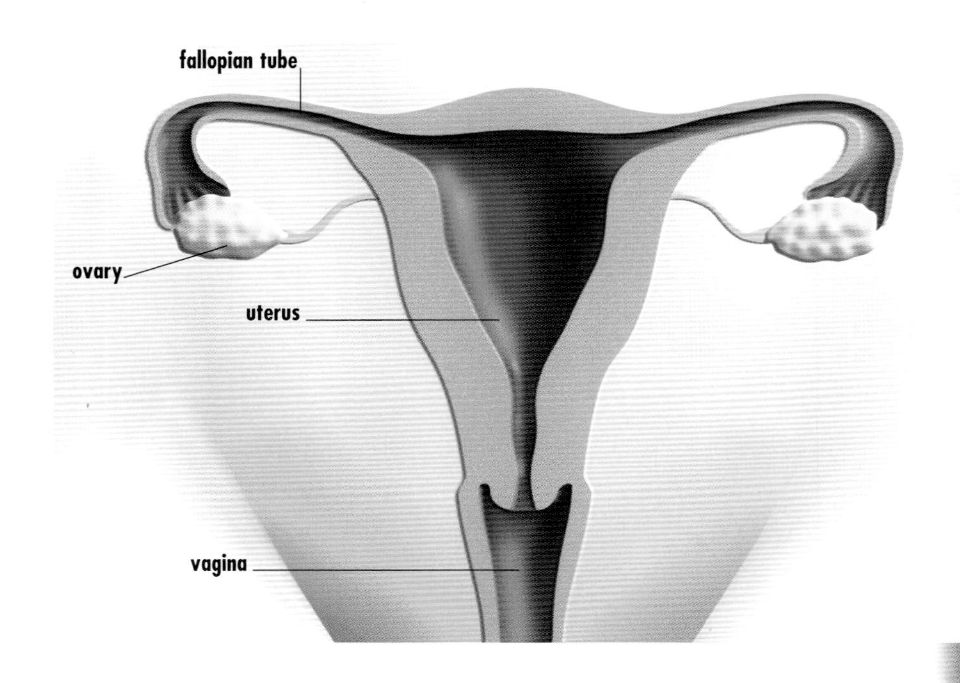

Female reproductive system

The organs of the female reproductive system – the vagina, uterus, fallopian tubes and ovaries – are located in the pelvis, the lowest part of the body's trunk. The vagina is a tube that links the system to the outside, and through which a baby is born. It leads to the uterus, a hollow organ with a muscular wall that protects and nurtures the baby as it develops inside the mother's body. The top of the uterus connects to a pair of fallopian tubes ending in funnel-shaped openings that partially surround the almond-sized ovaries.

Monthly cycles

Each month, between her teens and early fifties, a woman's reproductive (menstrual) cycle prepares her body for pregnancy. Each cycle lasts around 28 days. In an ovary, a few immature eggs start to mature within bag-like follicles. But only one egg ripens fully. Around day 14, it bursts out of its follicle into a fallopian tube. This is called ovulation. If the egg is fertilized by a sperm, the lining of the uterus thickens to receive it, and the egg will develop into a baby. But if fertilization does not take place the lining is shed through the vagina during a period (menstruation).

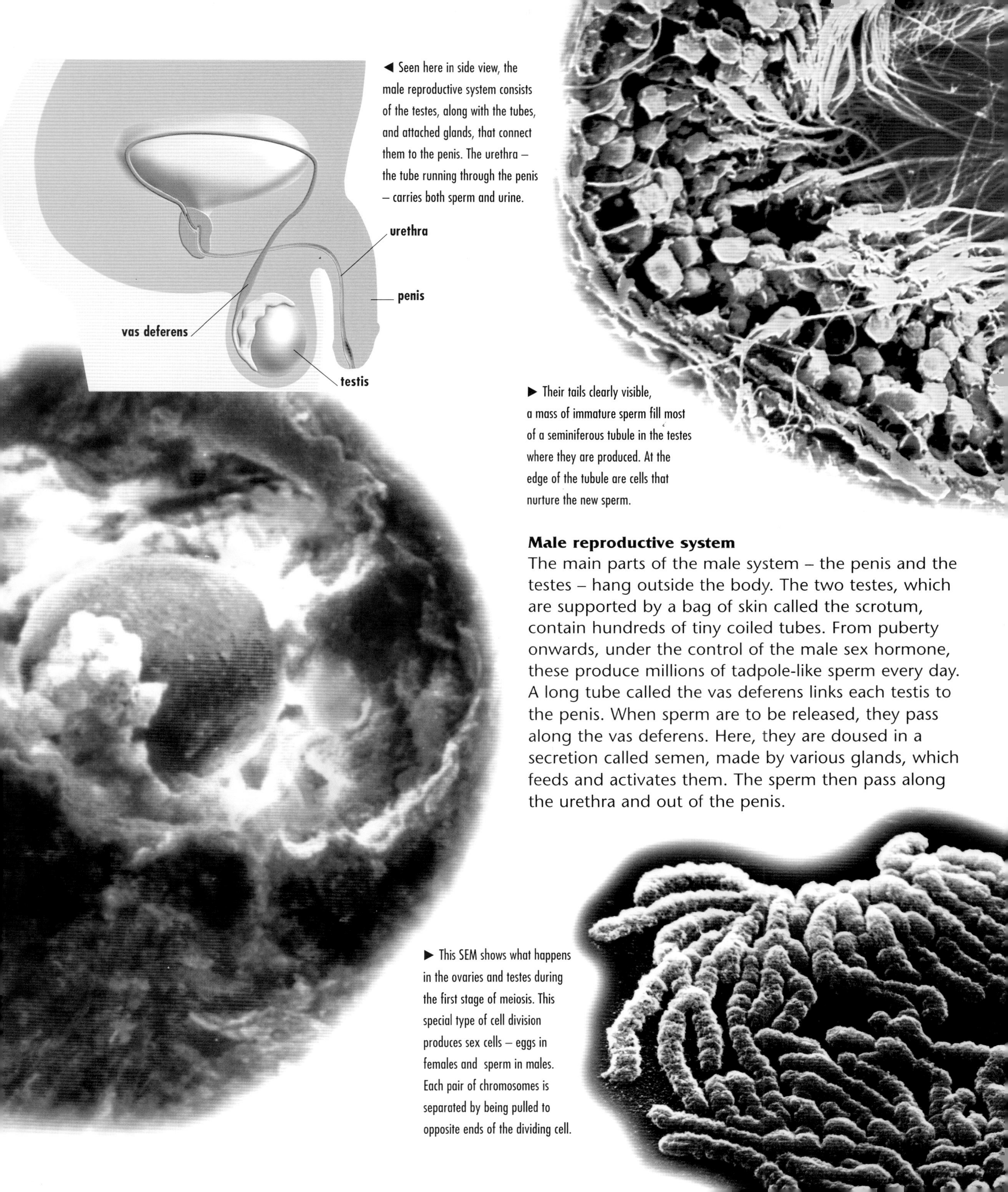

◀ Seen here in side view, the male reproductive system consists of the testes, along with the tubes, and attached glands, that connect them to the penis. The urethra – the tube running through the penis – carries both sperm and urine.

▶ Their tails clearly visible, a mass of immature sperm fill most of a seminiferous tubule in the testes where they are produced. At the edge of the tubule are cells that nurture the new sperm.

Male reproductive system

The main parts of the male system – the penis and the testes – hang outside the body. The two testes, which are supported by a bag of skin called the scrotum, contain hundreds of tiny coiled tubes. From puberty onwards, under the control of the male sex hormone, these produce millions of tadpole-like sperm every day. A long tube called the vas deferens links each testis to the penis. When sperm are to be released, they pass along the vas deferens. Here, they are doused in a secretion called semen, made by various glands, which feeds and activates them. The sperm then pass along the urethra and out of the penis.

▶ This SEM shows what happens in the ovaries and testes during the first stage of meiosis. This special type of cell division produces sex cells – eggs in females and sperm in males. Each pair of chromosomes is separated by being pulled to opposite ends of the dividing cell.

girl boy

▲ Eggs always carry an X sex chromosome, but sperm can carry either an X or a Y chromosome. An egg fertilized by an X-carrying sperm produces a girl (XX), while a Y-carrying sperm produces a boy (XY).

◀ This sperm (coloured purple) is burrowing into an egg. Sperm compete to get through the egg's zona pellucida (the 'fluffy' layer surrounding the egg) and penetrate its cell membrane in order to fertilize the egg.

Growing inside

All humans begin life at fertilization as a single cell, the fertilized egg. As a man's sperm and a woman's egg are united, the 23 chromosomes carried by each combine to form the working set of 46 chromosomes needed to build and operate a new, unique human being. From fertilization to birth takes around nine months. The fertilized egg divides repeatedly to form trillions of cells that grow and are shaped into a living human inside the mother's uterus.

A life begins

During sexual intercourse, millions of sperm from the man are introduced into the woman's vagina. These sperm swim into her uterus but only the strongest few hundred reach her fallopian tubes. If they arrive around the same time that an ovary releases an egg, fertilization will occur. Sperm mass around the egg, all trying to penetrate its outer layers. Eventually one succeeds – its tail falls off, and its head (containing its nucleus) fuses with the nucleus of the egg. The fertilized egg now travels towards the uterus.

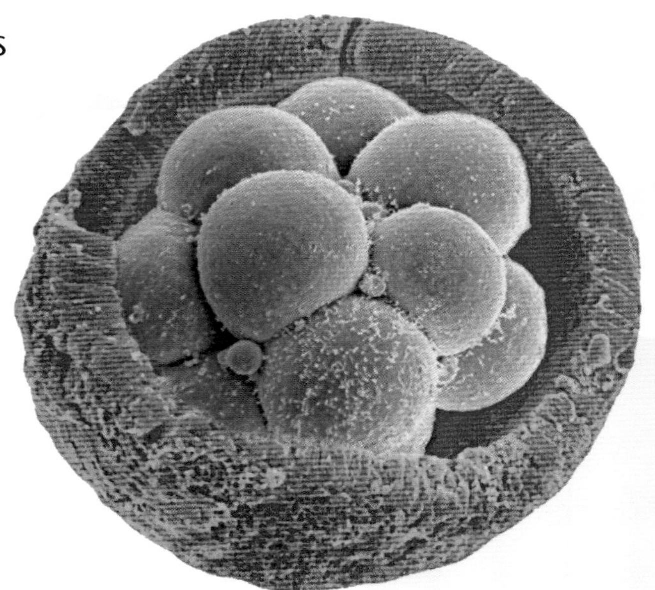

▲ Three days after fertilization, a fertilized egg has divided repeatedly to form a solid ball of 16 cells (coloured blue). The outer layer (red) is the remains of the zona pellucida that surrounded the egg.

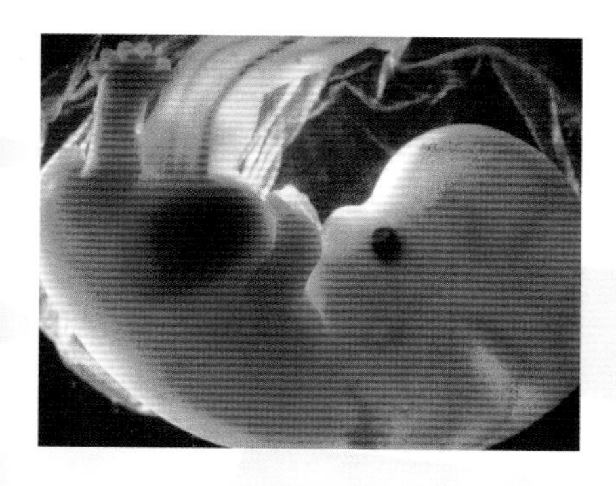

◀ At seven weeks old, the embryo is the size of a small strawberry. Its heart is beating, its main organs are present, and its limbs are growing. The umbilical cord (top left) links embryo and placenta.

From embryo to fetus

During its journey along the fallopian tubes, the fertilized egg divides repeatedly. After about a week, a hollow ball of cells called an embryo has formed. This reaches the uterus and sinks into its soft lining, signalling the start of pregnancy. Eight weeks after fertilization, a tiny human called a fetus has been formed. Pregnancy continues for 38 to 40 weeks. During this time the fetus is nurtured by oxygen and food that are supplied by a spongy disk called a placenta. This grows inside the uterus.

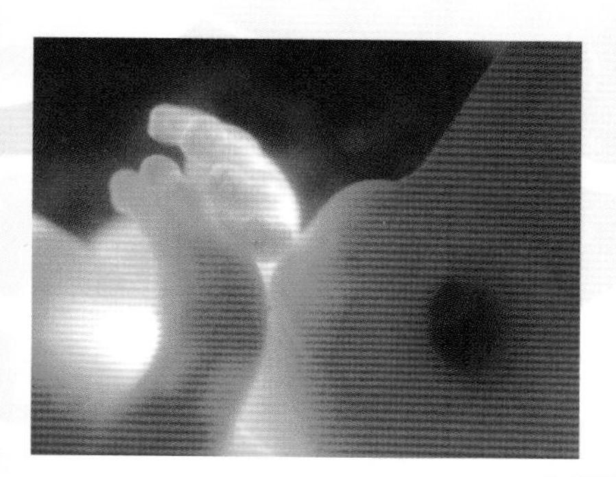

◀ The 10-week-old fetus is about 6cm long from head to buttocks. The limbs, which were once paddle-shaped, now have distinct fingers and toes. The large head accommodates the rapidly growing brain.

Shared inheritance

Women generally give birth to just one baby at a time. But one in 70 pregnancies results in either identical or fraternal (non-identical) twins. Identical twins are the result of a single fertilized egg splitting into two cells that separate and develop independently. They share the same genes, so they are always the same sex, and resemble each other very closely. Fraternal twins come about when two eggs are released at the same time by one or both ovaries and are then fertilized by different sperm. The resulting twins may be the same or different sexes, and are no more alike genetically than any other sisters or brothers.

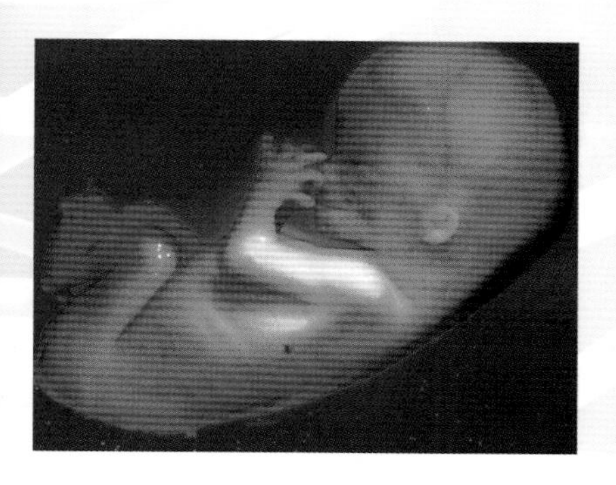

◀ At 15 weeks after fertilization, the fetus is around 14cm long. Its head, which has fully developed lips, eyelids and external ears, is large, although the limbs are now more in proportion.

▼ Identical twins, like these two girls, look amazingly similar and often share the same interests. However, because each twin has slightly different life experiences as she grows up, they will develop their own unique personalities.

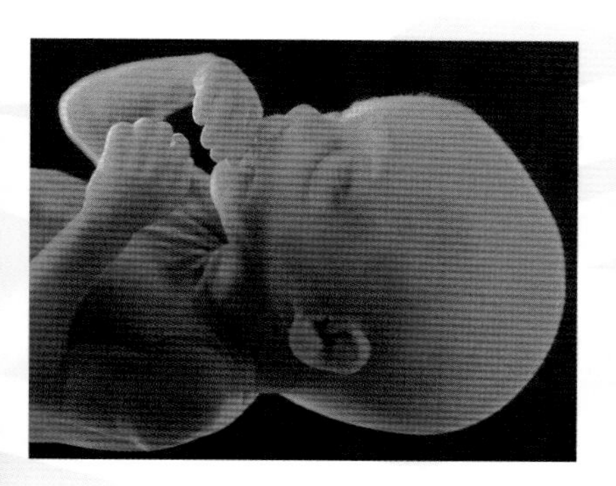

◀ At 20 weeks old, the fetus is about 19cm long and is visibly human. Its movements are now strong enough to be felt by its mother, and it will soon be able to hear sounds.

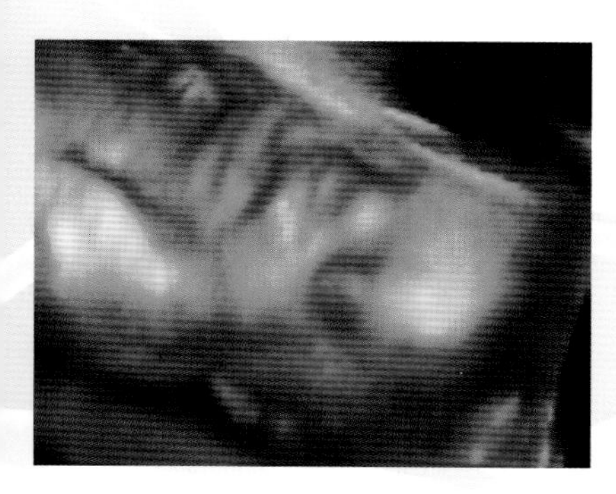

◀ This 3-D ultrasound scan shows a fetus at around 29 weeks, about nine or 10 weeks before birth. It is now about 30cm long, and gains weight rapidly as fat builds up below the skin.

Life story

Any of us who lives to a ripe old age goes through a fixed sequence of stages – birth, infancy, childhood, adolescence, adulthood and old age. These stages have defined human life since the evolution of our earliest ancestors. Although learning and growth is most rapid in the earliest years, life is a continuous process of mental and physical change. Ageing is inevitable, but its effects can often be lessened by a healthy lifestyle.

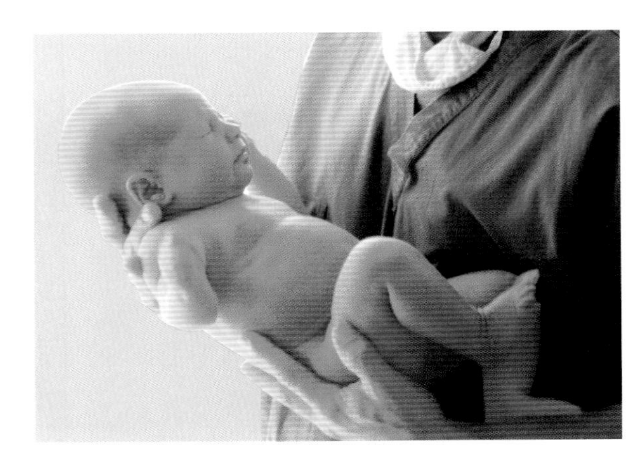

▲ This baby has just been born and is about to begin its journey through life. It has emerged from the warm, dark environment of its mother's uterus to the light and sounds of the outside world.

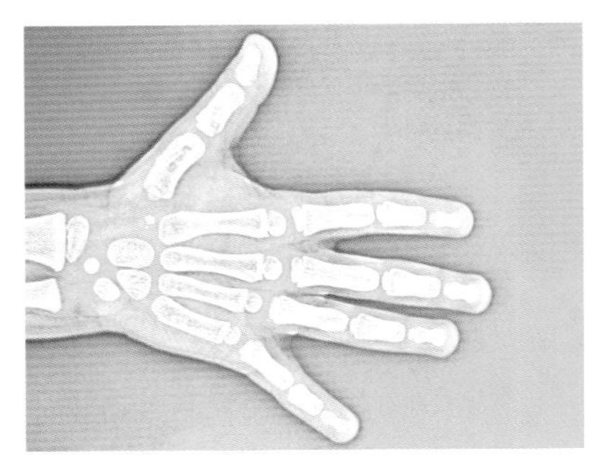

◀ These two X-rays compare the hands of a three-year-old child (above) and a 13-year-old teenager (below). The child's hand shows spaces between bones where the cartilage has not been replaced by bone. In the teenager's hand, the bones are almost fully grown.

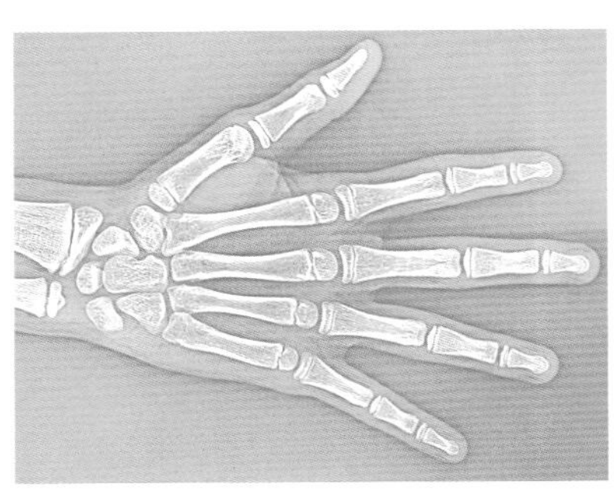

▶ A younger person, if they are fit and healthy, has a taut skin and, usually, a head of thick hair. Although they are ageing slowly at this time, the signs of ageing do not really appear until their fifties.

Birth and childhood

Infancy, the first 12 months after birth, is a time of rapid development and growth. As children enter their second year, they understand simple words and might be able to take a few steps. By the age of two they are beginning to put sentences together, and by the age of five they have begun to read and write. The body continues to change and grow throughout childhood. The cartilage that makes up part of the skeleton at birth is gradually replaced by bone. During childhood, billions of nerve cells, already present in the brain at birth, form connections with one another. This produces a powerful communication and control network.

Adolescence and puberty

With the teenage years comes adolescence, the period that separates childhood from adulthood. The start of adolescence is signalled by puberty, the physical changes triggered by sex hormones. In girls, puberty begins around the age of 11. It starts about two years later in boys. Both sexes experience rapid growth. In girls, the hips widen, breasts develop, pubic and armpit hair appears and periods begin. In boys, the body becomes more muscular, facial hair grows, the voice breaks and sperm production starts. With so many changes happening at once, adolescence can be a challenging time for many individuals.

► During adolescence, teenagers become more independent as they leave childhood behind. During this period, important friendships are formed and physical changes occur which make a person sexually mature.

▼ As a person ages, their skin becomes less elastic, or stretchy, so wrinkles and lines appear. The hair thins and becomes greyer as it loses its pigment, or colouring.

Adulthood

Between 18 and 20 years old, the body stops growing but it will continue to be maintained by its in-built repair system. Young adults complete their education and start their careers. Many find partners with whom they may have children. Brain cells continue to make new connections, although this happens at a slower rate than during childhood. The signs of ageing include wrinkles and lines appearing on the skin, hair turning grey and hearing becoming less sensitive. Many people have to start wearing glasses. After the age of 60, there is also a great chance of memory loss and the bones becoming weaker.

► During their twenties and thirties, many people start a family. The family provides a protective unit in which children can develop.

SUMMARY OF CHAPTER 1: PAST AND PRESENT

Human beings

The first humans appeared in Africa around five million years ago. These ancient ancestors were capable of walking on two legs, freeing their hands for other activities. Over the next few million years, many human species evolved but most branches of our family tree were dead ends. Only one human species – *Homo sapiens* – remains alive today. Over the course of evolution, the human brain grew considerably larger. Humans learned how to solve complex problems, use language and to express themselves through art. Their natural curiosity drove humans to discover more about themselves, something that continues to this day.

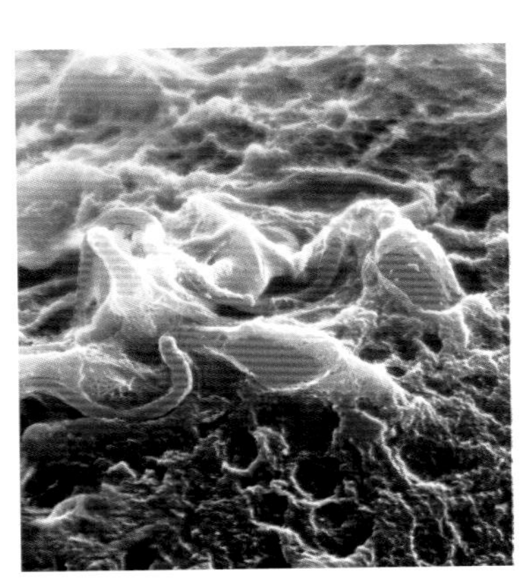

Sperm (coloured orange) attempting to penetrate the outer layer of an egg.

Body structure

In earlier times the only means of looking inside a living body was to cut it open. Nowadays we use modern technology such as CT or MRI scanning to produce images of the inside of the body. We know that the body is made up of trillions of cells organised into tissues. These form organs such as the heart or lungs. The body's systems, which work together to produce a whole body, are made up of linked organs.

New generations

If we did not reproduce, humans would soon die out as a species. Every body cell contains instructions called genes for making a human. The instructions are contained in the DNA that makes up chromosomes. As adults we produce sex cells that contain half of our chromosomes. When male and female sex cells meet at fertilization, their chromosomes unite. The fertilized egg, which has a full set of chromosomes, will grow and develop into a new baby. Once born, that baby will go through the same life stages that humans have experienced since we first appeared.

Go further...

Travel through the incredible journey of human evolution at:
www.becominghuman.org

Look at a wide range of historical illustrations of the body, including those by Vesalius at:
www.nlm.nih.gov/exhibition/dreamanatomy/da_gallery.html

Follow the process of fertilization step-by-step at:
www.uchsc.edu/ltc/Fertilization.html

See animations that show how DNA works at:
www.dnai.org/index.htm

KFK: Genes & DNA by Richard Walker (Kingfisher, 2003)

Anatomist
Studies the structure of the human body.

Geneticist
Studies how genes are passed on from one generation to the next, and what effects they have.

Medical artist
Artist who specializes in producing images of human anatomy.

Palaeoanthropologist
Studies the fossil remains of ancient humans to learn about our ancestors.

Radiologist
Doctor who diagnoses disease by interpreting X-rays, CT scans and other images.

Visit *Our Place in Evolution* at The Natural History Museum, Cromwell Road, London, SW7 5BD, UK
Telephone: +44 (0) 20 7942 5011
www.nhm.ac.uk

See Rembrandt's painting *The Anatomy Lesson of Dr Nicolaes Tulp* in the Hague:
The Mauritshuis Museum, Korte Vijverberg 8, NL 2513 AB Den Haag, The Netherlands
Telephone: +31 (0) 70 302 3456
www.mauritshuis.nl

Find out more about genes and DNA, and human history at the *Who am I?* gallery at The Science Museum, Exhibition Road, London, SW7 2DD
Telephone: +44 (0) 870 870 4868
www.sciencemuseum.org.uk

Seen in side view, this computer illustration of a skeleton reveals the remarkable flexibility of the arms and legs when a person is running fast.

CHAPTER 2

Body in action

Picture the scene. A person goes for a walk, sees clouds drifting across the sky, hears birds singing, thinks about dinner and remembers that they should have been home an hour earlier. All or parts of this experience could have happened to any one of us. And if it did, we would probably take it for granted. However, for us to be able to move, see, hear, think and remember, as well as every other task performed by the body, requires an incredibly complex interaction of body systems. The simplest of movements requires muscles to tug at the flexible bony framework that supports our body. Millions of electrical signals speed around the wiring of the nervous system each second to generate and fine tune those movements, and to make us feel, think and be ourselves.

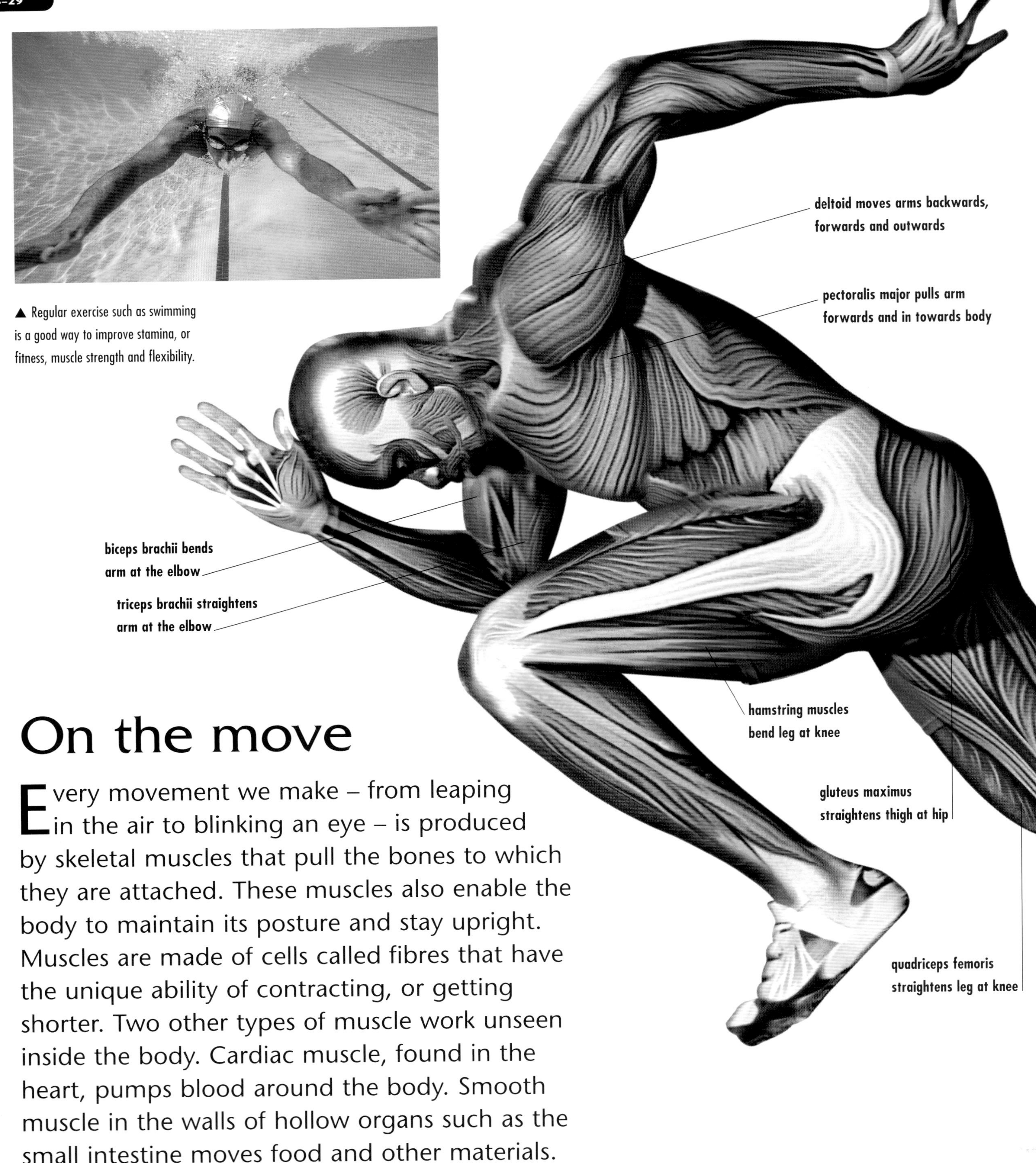

▲ Regular exercise such as swimming is a good way to improve stamina, or fitness, muscle strength and flexibility.

On the move

Every movement we make – from leaping in the air to blinking an eye – is produced by skeletal muscles that pull the bones to which they are attached. These muscles also enable the body to maintain its posture and stay upright. Muscles are made of cells called fibres that have the unique ability of contracting, or getting shorter. Two other types of muscle work unseen inside the body. Cardiac muscle, found in the heart, pumps blood around the body. Smooth muscle in the walls of hollow organs such as the small intestine moves food and other materials.

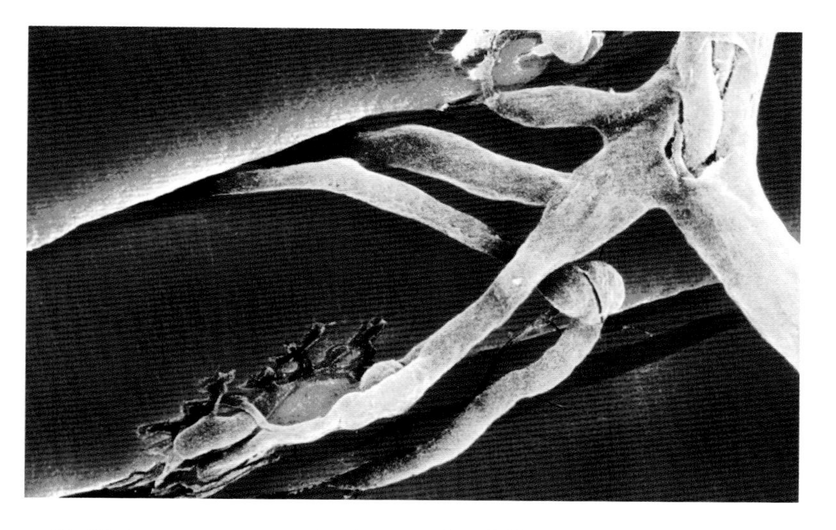

▲ This SEM shows a motor neuron (coloured green) and muscle fibres (red). Nerve impulses passing from neuron to muscle cause the fibres to contract, which in turn pull bones to produce movement.

From muscle to fibre

Some 650 skeletal muscles clothe the skeleton and give the body shape. They are arranged in layers and this provides strength, support and flexibility. Each muscle is made up of bundles of long cells called fibres. Within each fibre are smaller units called myofibrils which contain filaments that make the muscle contract. Blood vessels snake around the fibres to supply energy-rich glucose and oxygen.

◀ This athlete is using some of the body's major skeletal muscles. Muscles are given Latin names related to one or more of their features. 'Deltoid', for example, means triangular, while 'maximus' means largest.

gastrocnemius bends foot downwards

Getting shorter

Most movements, which are controlled by the brain, happen automatically without us thinking about it. Nerve impulses, or signals, travel from the brain to muscles along cells called motor neurons. When a nerve impulse enters a muscle, it causes the filaments to slide over each other, making the fibre, and the muscle, shorter. The contraction finishes when the nerve impulses stop. This process requires energy and releases heat as a waste product. Regular exercise, such as swimming and running, increases the size of muscle fibres, and of the blood vessels that supply them, which makes them more efficient.

In opposition

Muscles are connected to bones by tough cord or sheet-like extensions called tendons. Each muscle extends between two bones across the joint between them. Muscles only perform work when they pull during contraction. To move bones in opposite directions, muscles are arranged in groups with opposing actions. In the upper arm, for example, the biceps brachii muscle contracts, pulling the forearm bones towards the humerus (upper arm bone). This action bends the arm at the elbow. The triceps brachii, at the back of the upper arm, opposes that action. With the biceps relaxed, the triceps contracts to straighten the arm.

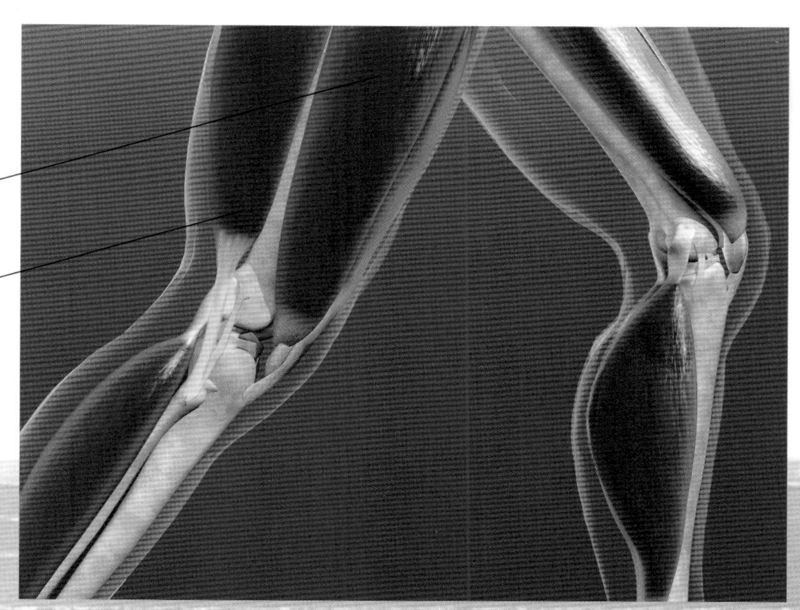

▲ Muscles cannot push, so most of the body's skeletal muscles work in pairs, each pulling bones in the opposite direction. The powerful quadriceps femoris muscle in the front of the thigh straightens the leg at the knee, while the hamstring muscles at the rear of the thigh bend the knee.

Bony framework

Without the support of its skeletal system – a living framework of bones, ligaments and cartilage – your body would collapse into a shapeless heap. The skeleton is built from 206 bones that are not, contrary to popular belief, dry and dusty. Bones are moist organs, supplied with blood and nerves. Lightweight and amazingly strong, they constantly change their shape and are able to repair themselves if damaged. As well as supporting the body, the skeleton protects soft organs such as the brain and heart. It also makes the body flexible because bones meet at joints that allow movement.

▲ This MRI scan of a knee joint, the body's largest joint, shows (in blue) the ends of the femur (upper bone) and tibia (lower bone). Between them is a space containing lubricating fluid. Tough straps called ligaments hold the bones together.

Strong and light

Incredibly, a living bone is as strong as a steel rod of the same size but is five times lighter. This combination of strength with lightness – an average adult skeleton weighs just 10kg – is down to a bone's structure. Bones are made from calcium salts that give them hardness, and fibres of the protein collagen, that gives them the strength and elasticity to withstand sudden twists and jolts. Each bone has an outer layer of dense compact bone tissue. Underneath this is a lighter network of rigid struts, called spongy bone. The spaces between these struts are filled with bone marrow. Bone cells constantly reshape the bones to maintain maximum strength and also repair bones if they fracture.

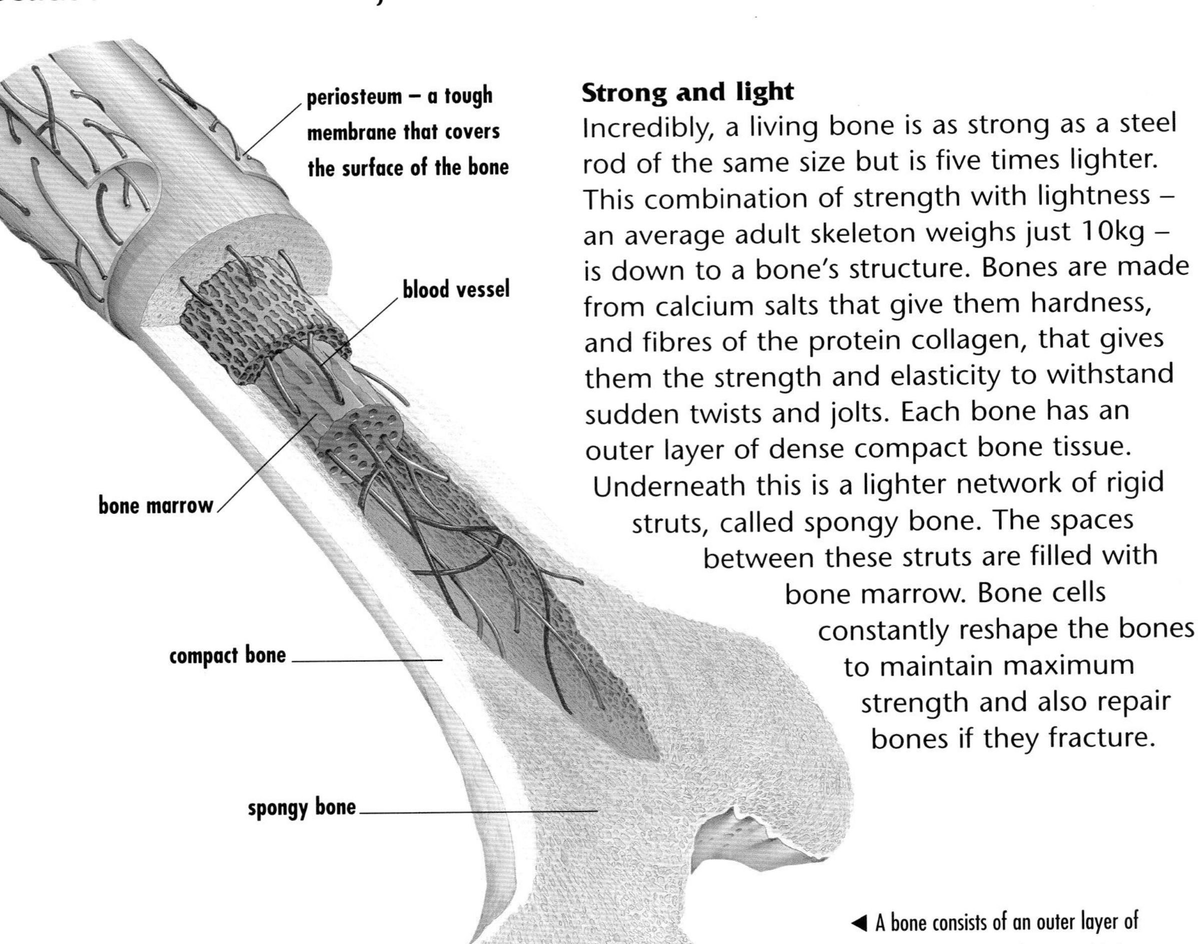

◀ A bone consists of an outer layer of hard compact bone and a core of lighter spongy bone. The central cavity contains bone marrow which manufactures millions of blood cells every second.

▲ These two SEMs show the structure of the two different types of bone tissue. Spongy bone (top) consists of struts and spaces. Compact bone (above) is made of parallel bony tubes, each surrounding a central canal that carries blood vessels and nerves.

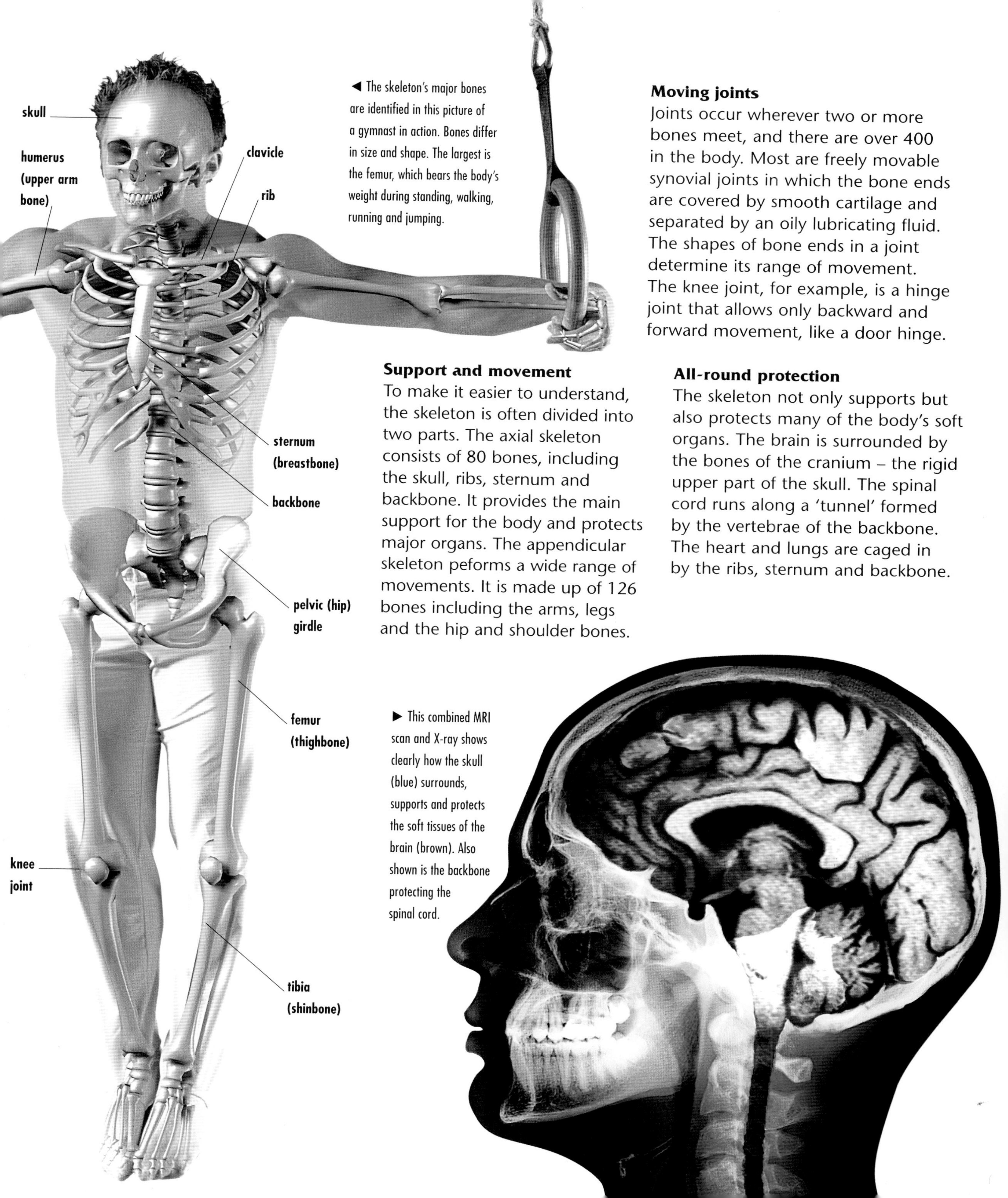

◀ The skeleton's major bones are identified in this picture of a gymnast in action. Bones differ in size and shape. The largest is the femur, which bears the body's weight during standing, walking, running and jumping.

Moving joints

Joints occur wherever two or more bones meet, and there are over 400 in the body. Most are freely movable synovial joints in which the bone ends are covered by smooth cartilage and separated by an oily lubricating fluid. The shapes of bone ends in a joint determine its range of movement. The knee joint, for example, is a hinge joint that allows only backward and forward movement, like a door hinge.

Support and movement

To make it easier to understand, the skeleton is often divided into two parts. The axial skeleton consists of 80 bones, including the skull, ribs, sternum and backbone. It provides the main support for the body and protects major organs. The appendicular skeleton peforms a wide range of movements. It is made up of 126 bones including the arms, legs and the hip and shoulder bones.

All-round protection

The skeleton not only supports but also protects many of the body's soft organs. The brain is surrounded by the bones of the cranium – the rigid upper part of the skull. The spinal cord runs along a 'tunnel' formed by the vertebrae of the backbone. The heart and lungs are caged in by the ribs, sternum and backbone.

▶ This combined MRI scan and X-ray shows clearly how the skull (blue) surrounds, supports and protects the soft tissues of the brain (brown). Also shown is the backbone protecting the spinal cord.

In control

With so much going on inside the body, we need ways of keeping everything co-ordinated and under control. Our nervous system is in charge of most body activities. It works at lightning speed, allowing us to think and feel while controlling our movements and many internal workings. Our endocrine, or hormonal, system works more slowly and with longer-term effects. It is involved in a number of processes including reproduction, growth and protection against stress.

◀ Every action taken by this goalkeeper is controlled by the nervous system. It allows him to see the ball and to judge its speed and position with great accuracy. It also instructs the muscles to launch him off the ground and into the right position to make a perfect save.

▲ This computer-generated image zooms in on a few of the billions of neurons inside the brain. Each neuron has a cell body with fine filaments called dendrites. These receive impulses from other neurons. The longer and thicker filaments, called axons or nerve fibres, carry impulses to the next neuron.

Nervous system

The nervous system reaches out to just about every part of the body. Its command centre is the central nervous system (CNS) – the brain and spinal cord. A massive network of cable-like nerves relays nerve messages between the body and the CNS. The CNS receives a constant stream of information about what is happening inside and outside the body from sensors. It also sends out instructions to muscles and organs.

Neurons

Billions of neurons, or nerve cells, are key to the operation of the nervous system. These highly specialized cells transmit weak electrical signals called impulses. The signals travel at speeds of up to 360km/h – that's from big toe to spinal cord in 1/100th of a second. In the CNS, neurons are massed together with multiple connections to form an incredibly complex network.

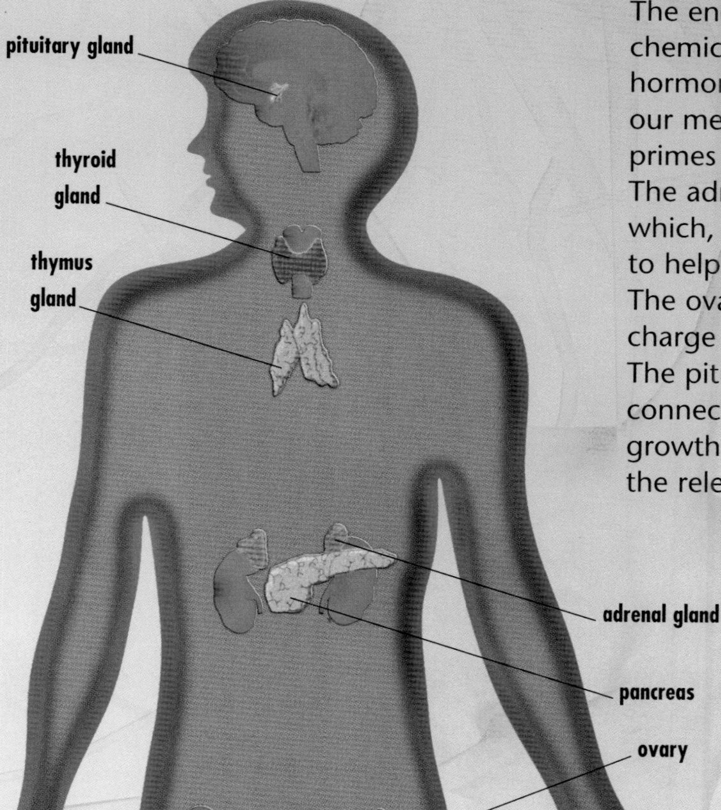

◄ This body map of a female shows the main endocrine organs found in the body. In males, the ovaries are replaced by the two testes.

Hormones

The endocrine glands release chemical messages called hormones. The thyroid controls our metabolic rate. The thymus primes immune system cells. The adrenals release adrenalin which, unusually, works rapidly to help us respond to danger. The ovaries and testes are in charge of reproduction. The pituitary gland, which is connected to the brain, makes growth hormone and controls the release of other hormones.

Who am I?

Every time you wake up, you know automatically who you are from your own unique thoughts, emotions and memories. This feeling of 'self' is generated by the brain. Locked inside the skull, this soft, pink, wrinkled organ is the most complex thing known to humans. Exactly how it works is still largely a mystery. We do know, however, that each of the brain's 100 million neurons is connected to hundreds or thousands of other neurons. This creates a communication and processing network, far more complex than even the most advanced computer.

▶ Electrodes attached to this young woman's head measure the electrical activity in her brain as she sleeps. Brain activity is shown as an electroencephalogram (EEG) trace on a screen. Studies of brain activity have shown that during sleep we go through five different stages.

Brain features

The biggest part of the brain is the cerebrum. It has left and right halves, or hemispheres, which control their opposite side of the body. The thin outer layer of each hemisphere is called the cortex or grey matter. The cortex receives and processes information and also sends out instructions to the rest of the body. Sensory areas of the cortex receive infomation from sensors in, for example, the eyes, ears and skin so that we can experience the world around us. Motor areas instruct muscles to contract to move the body. Association areas analyze, interpret and store information, enabling us to learn, think, plan, create and be self-aware.

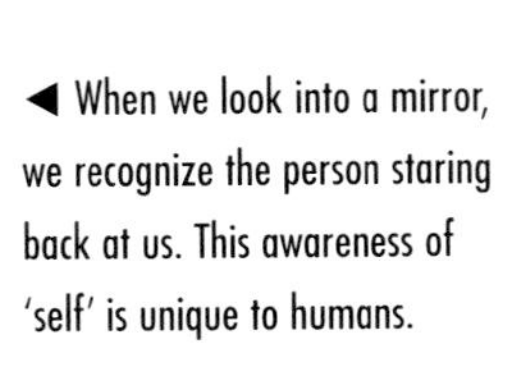

◀ When we look into a mirror, we recognize the person staring back at us. This awareness of 'self' is unique to humans.

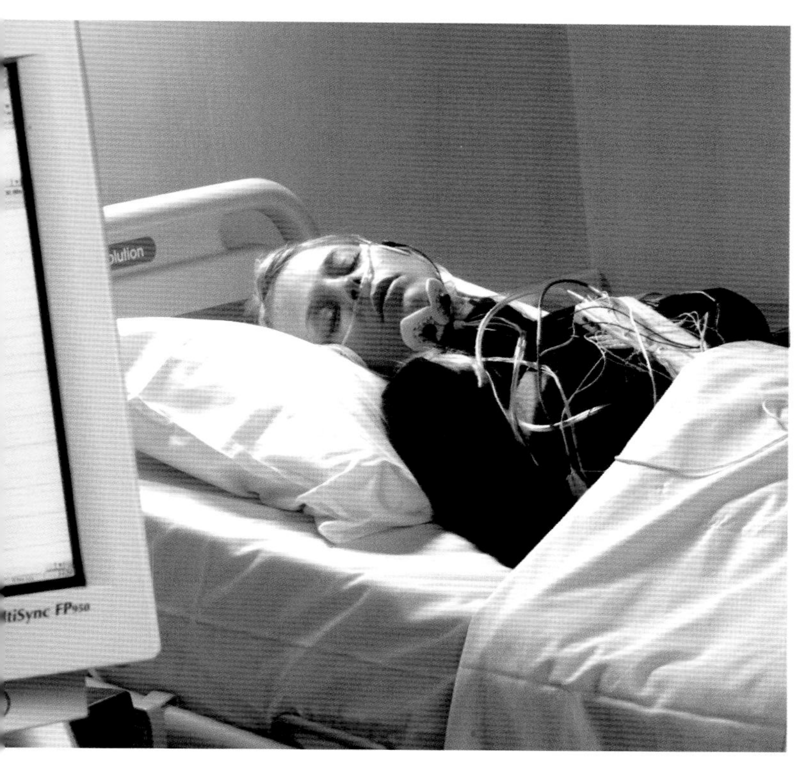

Sleep and dreams

An average person spends about one-third of their life asleep. When we are asleep, our awareness of the world 'switches off'. But that does not mean that our brains stop working. Recordings of electrical activity in the brain – known as brain waves – can be made using an electroencephalograph. The traces, or EEGs, it produces show that brain wave patterns change as we sleep. Throughout the night we go repeatedly from deep sleep to light sleep and back again. It is during periods of light sleep (also called REM sleep) that we dream.

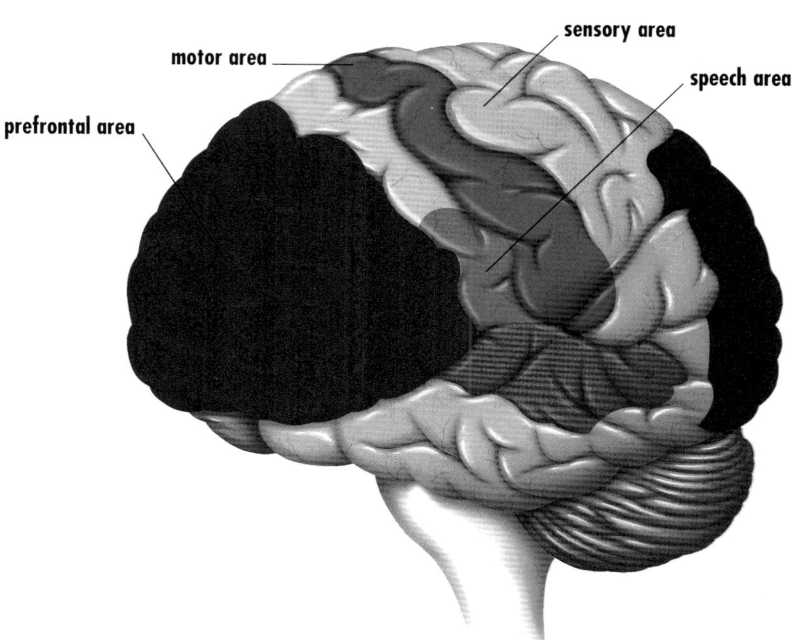

▲ The cerebrum is divided into areas that carry out different tasks. These include the motor area which triggers movement, the speech area which produces speech, and the sensory area which receives signals from skin. The prefrontal area is involved in thinking.

Memories, emotions and fears

Located deep inside our brain, the limbic system works with the cerebrum to give us memory and emotions. Without memory we would be unable to learn or be creative, or even recognize ourselves! Our short-term memory holds on to sights and sounds just long enough for us to act on them. Some of these events are stored by the hippocampus and shifted to our long-term memory. This allows us to recall words, faces and important experiences in our lives. Anger, happiness, pleasure and fear are just some of the emotions produced by the limbic system. Sometimes fear of a particular object or a situation may become greatly exaggerated in our minds. This is when a normal fear turns into a phobia.

◀ Just the sight of this tarantula is enough to make some people panic. That is because they suffer from arachnophobia, an irrational fear of spiders, and one of many phobias that may affect us.

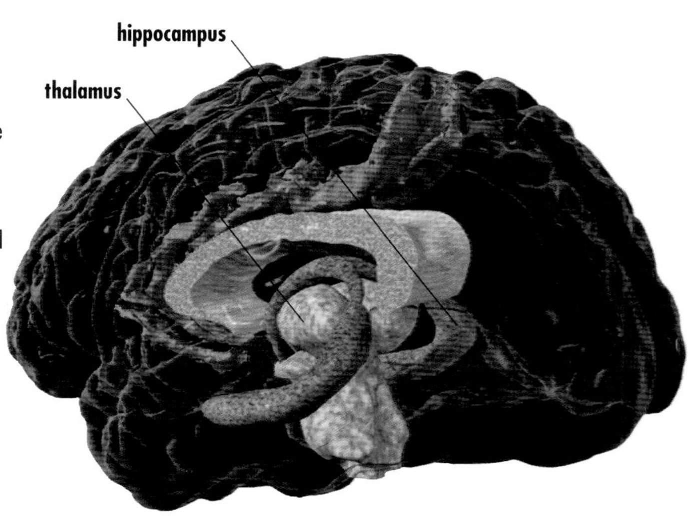

◀ This colour-coded 3-D MRI scan of the brain (from the left side) shows the limbic system, which controls the emotions. The thalamus relays signals from the rest of the body to the cortex. The hippocampus is involved in memory.

Person to person

Humans are social animals, so communicating with each other is really important. Whether we are interacting with one person or many, communication allows us to make others aware of our thoughts and emotions. We can also share and develop ideas and pass information down the generations. Controlled by various centres in the brain, human communication, the most sophisticated in the living world, takes different forms. Spoken and written language is unique to humans. Body language and facial expressions provide a huge range of signals about our mood.

▲ There is no mistaking the emotions displayed here. The body language of these football fans says it all. Raised arms, open mouths and big smiles all indicate that their team is winning.

▲ Writing systems vary from culture to culture. Chinese employs a logographic system that uses characters (above) to represent one word or part of a word. English uses an alphabetic system of letters to represent each vowel and consonant.

Using words
Language has enabled humans to make incredible cultural and technological progress over the past 10,000 years. Today over 5,000 languages are spoken in the world. Some, including Mandarin Chinese, English and Spanish, are used by billions of people. Written language enables us to keep records of our cultures and ideas. Speech, the most versatile form of language, means we can converse with one person or many people at the same time.

Making speech
Sounds are generated by two flaps called the vocal cords. These are found in the larynx, or voice box, and can open and close. Muscles in the larynx shorten the vocal cords and pull them together, like drawn curtains. Air from the lungs is pushed between the vocal cords in controlled bursts so that they vibrate and make sounds. Low-pitched sounds are produced by loose vocal cords, while high-pitched ones are made by tight ones. These sounds are modified by the lips and tongue to produce understandable speech. When they are not making sounds, the larynx muscles relax and the vocal cords open to allow the free passage of air. The whole process is controlled by a section of the left side of the brain called Broca's area. It sends instructions to the larynx and tongue.

Body language

The way we stand and position our limbs, the gestures we make, and our facial expressions – all of these make up our body language. As a means of communication it can be just as revealing as spoken words. Body language can convey whether we are lying or telling the truth, if we are interested or bored, and many other things. Facial expressions reveal feelings and emotions including fear, disgust, surprise and amusement. They are made by small muscles that pull on the skin to produce a range of expressions from a broad smile to a frown.

▼ When the vocal cords are closed (top), air from the lungs is forced through to produce sounds. To allow breathing, the vocal cords stay open (bottom).

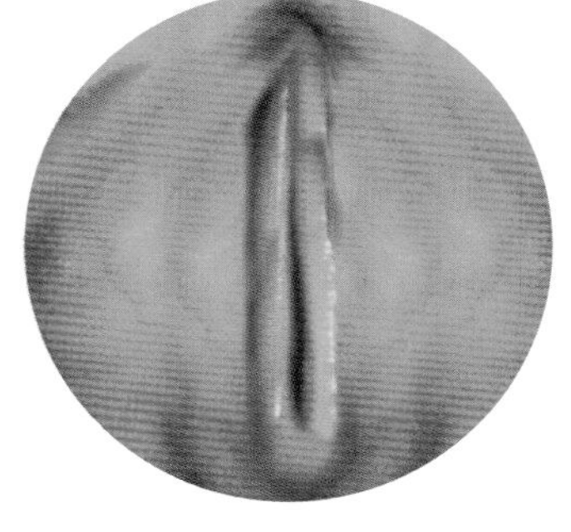

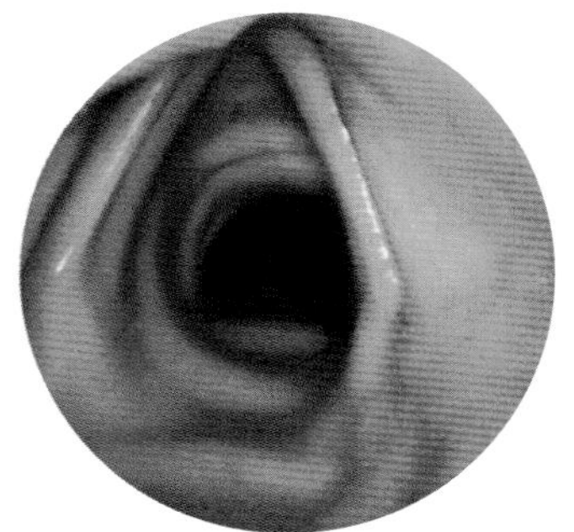

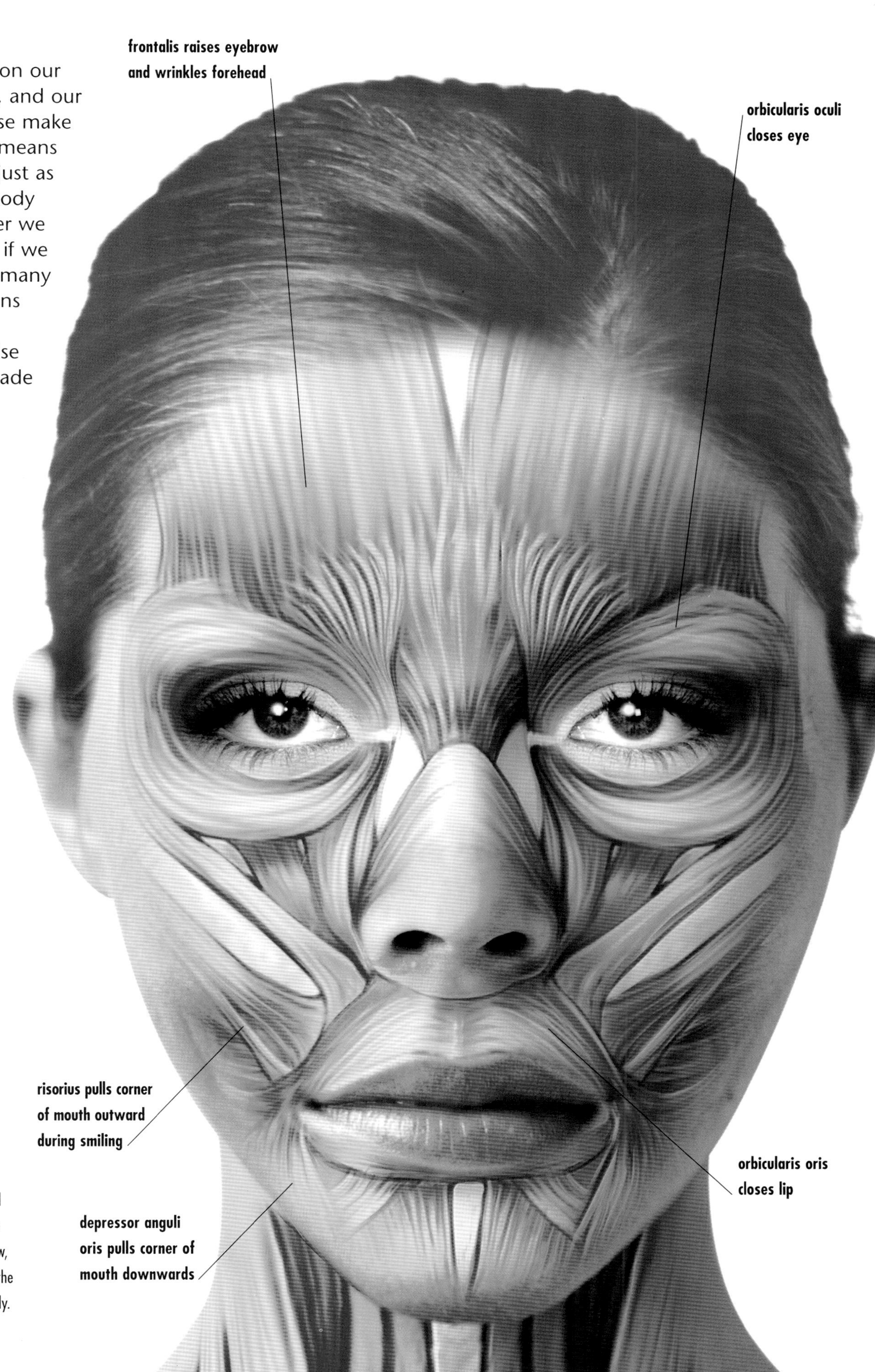

► Over 30 small muscles produce facial expressions. Most work in pairs, just like the muscles in the rest of the body. A few, however, such as the muscle that closes the eye during winking, can work individually.

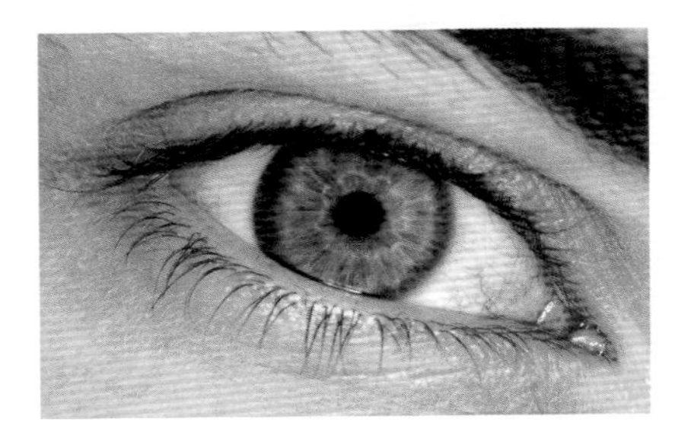

▲ Pupils dilate, or widen, in dim light (top) to let more light into the eye, and constrict, or narrow, in bright light (bottom) to prevent too much getting in.

▼ This SEM of the eye's retina shows its light-sensitive cells. Rods (green) work best in dim light, while cones (blue) detect colour. There are around 120 million rods spread throughout the retina. About 6.5 million cones are located mainly in the fovea, the area on which light is focussed when we look directly at an object.

Seeing the world

Our ability to read these words – and to appreciate much of what is happening around us – depends on vision. Many people mistakenly think that we 'see' with our eyes. In fact, the job our eyes do is to respond to light from our surroundings by firing off nerve impulses to the brain. In the brain, information from the eyes is interpreted as full-colour, three-dimensional images. It is these images that we 'see'. Built-in control systems allow the eyes automatically to focus light and to adjust the amount of light entering them.

Inside the eye

Apart from the front of the eye, where the transparent cornea allows light in, the surface of each eyeball is covered by a tough, white coat called the sclera.

The eye's interior is divided by the lens. In front of the lens, the coloured iris surrounds a central opening, the pupil. Behind the lens, the eyeball is lined with the thin retina, a layer packed with photoreceptors, or light-sensitive cells. About 85 per cent of each eyeball lies hidden, encased in a protective socket in the skull, cushioned by pads of fat. Muscles connecting sclera and socket move the eyeball up, down and from side to side.

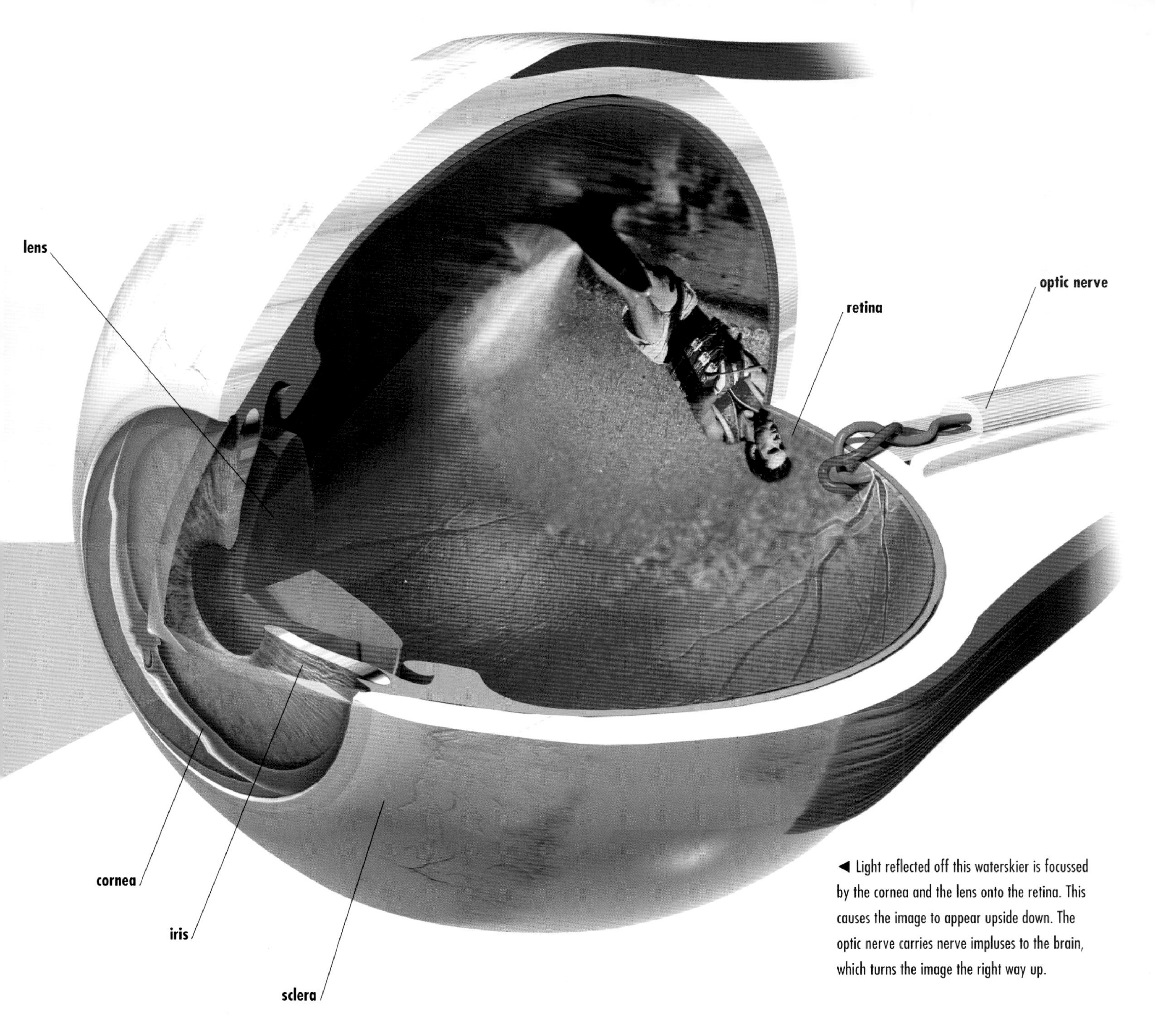

◀ Light reflected off this waterskier is focussed by the cornea and the lens onto the retina. This causes the image to appear upside down. The optic nerve carries nerve impluses to the brain, which turns the image the right way up.

In focus

Light rays reflected from an object, such as this waterskier in action (above), enter the eye through the cornea. The rays are refracted, or bent, by the cornea and lens to form a sharp, upside-down image on the retina. This houses millions of photoreceptors of two types – rods and cones. Rods detect black and white, while cones are tuned to provide detailed, colour vision. The adjustable lens changes shape to focus light rays from both near and distant objects. The iris controls the amount of light entering the eye by widening or narrowing the pupil.

Visual brain

When hit by light, a photoreceptor fires off a nerve impulse. This travels along the optic nerve to the visual area at the back of each hemisphere, or half, of the brain. Inside the visual areas, the stream of impulses from the eyes are turned into images. By comparing this information with what it saw a few seconds earlier, the brain creates a visual 'map' of our surroundings. Each eye has a slightly different view of the world. This is important for vision, as these differences are used by the brain to see objects in three dimensions, and also to let us judge distances.

Sounds and flavours

Hearing, smell and taste are key senses. Hearing enables us to identify a vast array of sounds, to understand speech and to appreciate music. The ears also contain sensors that help us to balance and stay upright. Our senses of smell and taste work closely together so we can enjoy the flavours of good food but avoid bad-tasting food that could cause us harm.

Hearing

Every source of sound – from a whining mosquito to a roaring jet engine – vibrates. This causes sound waves to travel through the air and enter the ear, where they make the eardrum vibrate. As a result, bones called ossicles, found in the middle ear, move in and out. These movements, in turn, create pressure waves in the shell-shaped cochlea. The vibrations here are relayed as nerve messages to the brain and the person hears the sound.

▼ V-shaped groups of 'hairs' are found in the cochlea. Vibration of these 'hairs' by incoming sound waves causes them to send messages to the brain.

Balance

The inner ear has two types of balance sensors. Three semi-circular canals detect rotation of the head. The utricle and saccule track both the position of the head and movement of the body. This information, together with messages from other parts of the body, is used by the brain to hold us balanced and upright.

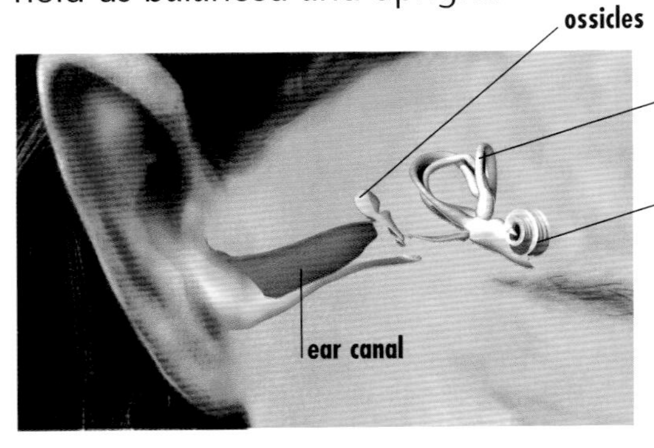

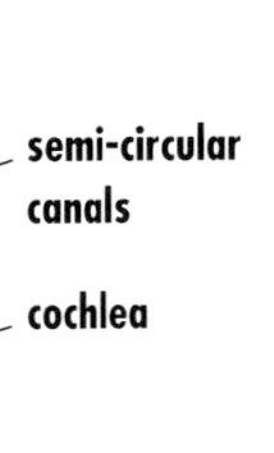

▲ This section through the side of the head shows the main parts of the ear. The ear flap, or pinna, directs sounds into the ear canal.

▶ Without a sense of balance, staying in this position would be impossible. Sensors in the ear and around the body, including the feet and joints, feed information to the brain. Then the brain sends instructions to the muscles that stop the body from falling over.

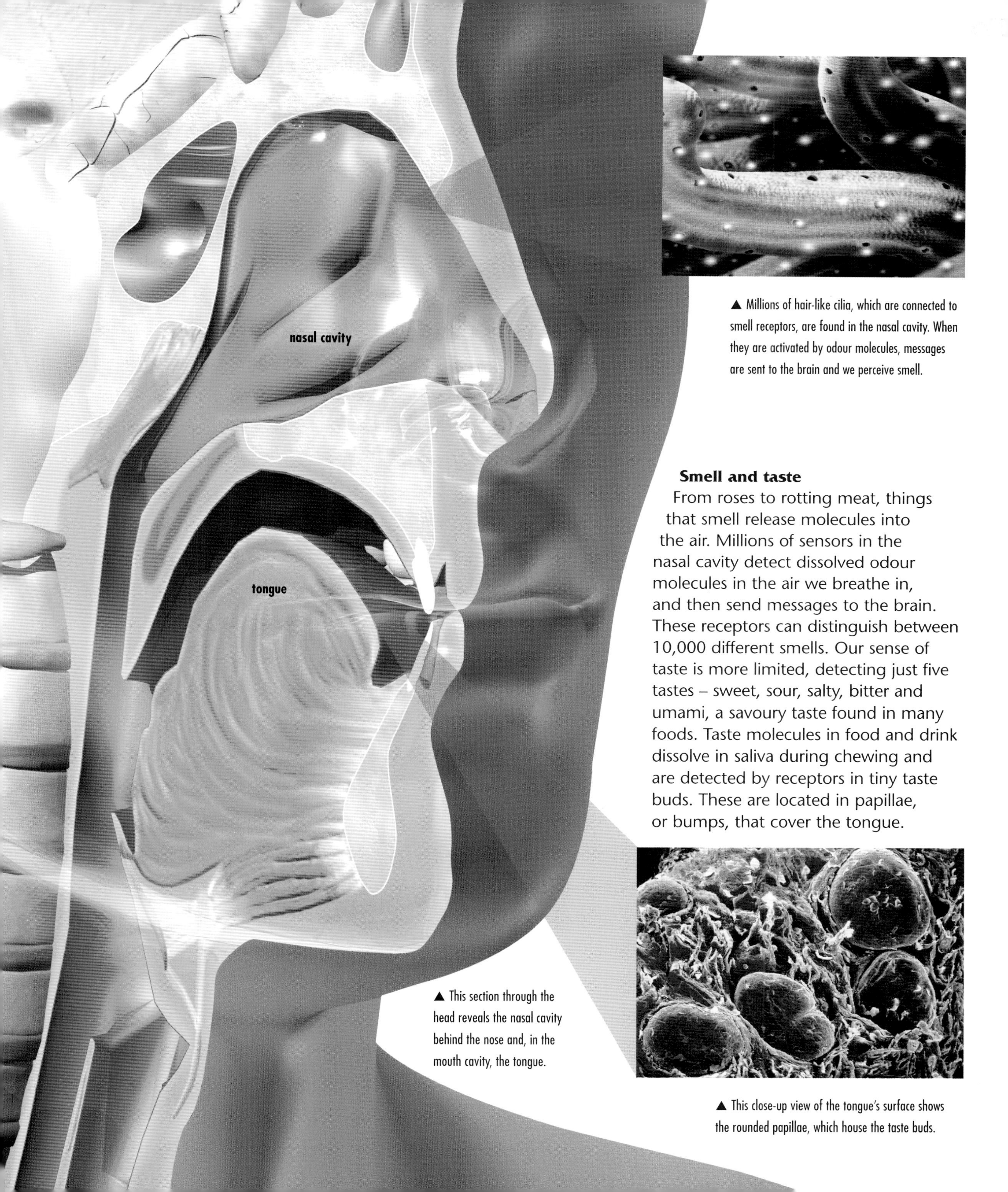

▲ Millions of hair-like cilia, which are connected to smell receptors, are found in the nasal cavity. When they are activated by odour molecules, messages are sent to the brain and we perceive smell.

Smell and taste

From roses to rotting meat, things that smell release molecules into the air. Millions of sensors in the nasal cavity detect dissolved odour molecules in the air we breathe in, and then send messages to the brain. These receptors can distinguish between 10,000 different smells. Our sense of taste is more limited, detecting just five tastes – sweet, sour, salty, bitter and umami, a savoury taste found in many foods. Taste molecules in food and drink dissolve in saliva during chewing and are detected by receptors in tiny taste buds. These are located in papillae, or bumps, that cover the tongue.

▲ This section through the head reveals the nasal cavity behind the nose and, in the mouth cavity, the tongue.

▲ This close-up view of the tongue's surface shows the rounded papillae, which house the taste buds.

SUMMARY OF CHAPTER 2: BODY IN ACTION

Moving framework

Our body is supported by a living scaffolding of bones clothed with a covering of muscles. The bones are organized into a flexible skeleton that forms a stable framework, as well as surrounding and protecting delicate internal organs. The skeleton also allows the body to move freely. Movement is achieved by skeletal muscles. The cells that form this muscle are long, cylindrical fibres that contract when instructed to do so by the arrival of a nerve impulse from the brain or spinal cord. Stretched across a joint, muscles pull on bones to move a particular body part. Regular exercise increases the efficiency of muscles and improves general body fitness. Other types of muscle make the heart beat and push fluids along hollow body organs.

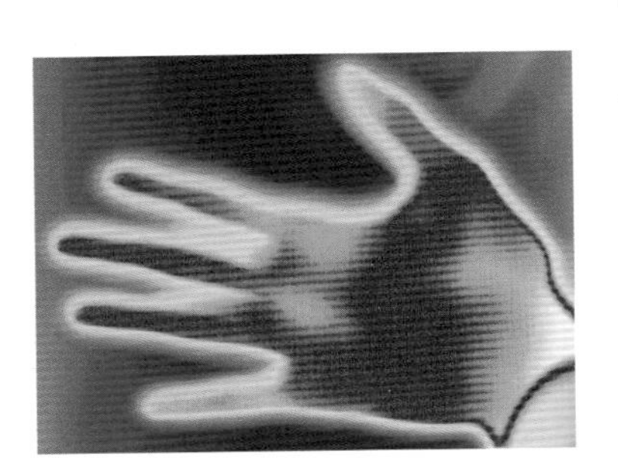

This thermogram reveals heat lost through the skin of the hand.

Brain at work

Our body movements would be jerky and unco-ordinated without the brain and nervous system. The brain controls muscle contraction by sending nerve impulses along nerves to the muscles. The brain also receives information from sensors in the eyes, skin and in other locations to keep it updated about conditions inside and outside the body. The brain processes this information and makes decisions about what action to take. The brain also allows us to think, imagine, communicate and to remember.

Sensing the world

Without our senses we would be unaware of the world around us. The eyes detect changes in light patterns from objects around us and send a constant stream of impulses to the brain. Here, the impulses are interpreted as images that we can see. Our ears pick up sound waves, turning them into nerve impulses that are sent to the brain. Taste and smell both detect chemicals in, respectively, food and in the air. Together, they allow us to enjoy the flavours of food and reject anything that might cause us harm.

Go further...

Investigate and interact with the nervous system, muscles and bones at:
www.bbc.co.uk/science/humanbody/body/index.shtml

Move a skeleton and find out lots more about muscles and joints at:
http://insideout.rigb.org/ri/anatomy/casing_the_joint/joints_explorer.html

Find out how to trick the brain at:
www.exploratorium.edu/exhibits

Learn about the benefits of exercise at:
www.kidshealth.org/kid/stay_healthy/fit/work_it_out.html

Body – An amazing tour of human anatomy by Robert Winston (Dorling Kindersley, 2005)

Neurologist
Specializes in diseases of the nervous system and the brain.

Ophthalmologist
Studies the eye and treats diseases and disorders that affect it.

Orthopaedic surgeon
Specializes in diagnosing and treating diseases and injuries that affect the bones.

Physiotherapist
Uses physical therapy such as massage or exercise to treat disease.

Psychologist
Studies the mind and human behaviour.

For more about the brain, visit: At-Bristol, Harbourside, Bristol, BS1 5DB, UK
Telephone: +44 (0) 845 345 1235
www.at-bristol.org.uk

For a hands-on experience of human biology and other sciences, visit:
The Exploratorium, The Palace of Fine Arts, 3601 Lyon Street, San Francisco CA 94123, USA
Telephone: +1 415 561 0308
www.exploratorium.edu

Discover the future of the brain at:
Human Lab, San Diego Museum of Man, 1350 El Prado, Balboa Park San Diego, CA 92101, USA
Telephone: +1 619 239 2001
www.abouthumanevolution.org

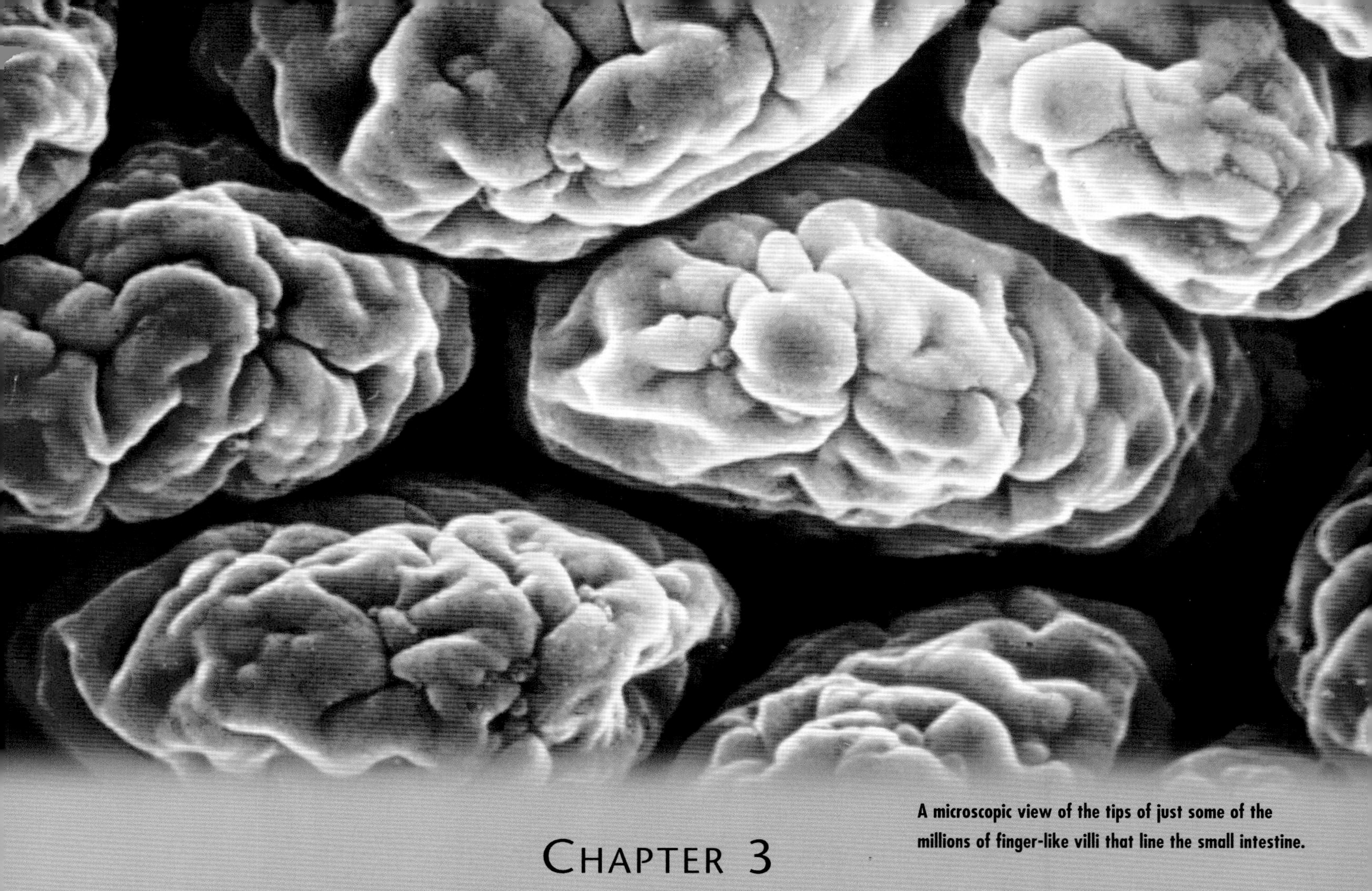

A microscopic view of the tips of just some of the millions of finger-like villi that line the small intestine.

CHAPTER 3

Supply and defence

Our bodies are finely-tuned machines that work non-stop, 24 hours a day. To keep up this punishing pace, the human body – or rather, its trillions of cells – needs to be serviced and protected at all times. Cells work at their best when conditions inside the body remain constant. They need to be kept warm, at around 37°C, and bathed in a fluid made up of just the right ingredients. Constant deliveries of glucose and oxygen are essential, because together they provide the energy that keeps the inner parts of each cell working. Waste generated by the busy body machine is whisked away and disposed of before it has time to upset cell activity and cause damage. For most of our lives, this incredibly complex system operates without any problems. Occasionally, however, the machine malfunctions because of disease. If this happens, the body's defences step in to protect its cells and halt disease in its tracks.

Feeding the body

Without a regular intake of food, our bodies cease to function. Food supplies us with the energy that runs our cells, powers our brain and gets us moving. Food contains the building blocks that enable us to grow and to repair our bodies. We need to consume a balanced mix of different food types to get all the essential substances called nutrients. To get food into our bodies we first use our teeth to cut it into pieces that can be swallowed.

▶ This food pyramid provides a guide to healthy eating. The different layers, from bottom to top, represent complex carbohydrates, fruit and vegetables, protein-rich foods, and finally, foods rich in fats, oils and sugar. For a balanced diet you should eat plenty from the bottom and very little from the top.

Essential nutrients
The food we eat every day contains three major groups of nutrients – carbohydrates, proteins and fats – as well as smaller amounts of vitamins and minerals. Carbohydrates provide us with energy, proteins are used to build and repair the body, as are fats which also provide an energy store. Vitamins and minerals are needed for the normal working of a healthy body. Eating vegetable fibre, or roughage, makes digestion more efficient. We also need to drink plenty of water because it makes up over half of the body.

Balanced diet
A balanced diet should have a broad mix of foods. If possible, the food should be fresh and not processed. We should eat plenty of fruit and vegetables, and not too much animal fat or refined sugar. Your body also needs essential vitamins, such as the B vitamins, found in fish, meat and eggs. Like vitamins, minerals help the body to grow and stay healthy. Minerals, such as calcium, can be found in dairy products and leafy green vegetables.

▼ Fresh fruit and vegetables are key ingredients of a healthy diet. Doctors and scientists recommend that we all eat at least five portions of fruit and vegetables daily. One portion could be, say, an apple or banana, or a handful of strawberries or carrot slices.

Obesity

People who are very overweight in relation to their height are termed 'obese'. Rates of obesity are increasing rapidly in both children and adults because many of us exercise too little and eat too much junk food, which contains a lot of fat and sugar. Obesity increases the possibility of developing many conditions including heart disease and arthritis. Avoiding obesity requires a healthy, balanced diet as well as regular exercise.

Teeth and chewing

To obtain the nutrients from food, we need to eat it. First, we have to break up food before swallowing it. This is the job of the teeth, which are anchored in the jawbones and tipped with hard enamel. Teeth come in various shapes and sizes. The incisors and canines at the front of the mouth grip and chop food, while the bigger premolars and molars further back crush and chew. Daily brushing of teeth removes plaque, a mixture of bacteria and old food. Left on the teeth, plaque will release acids that cause tooth decay.

► Magnified some 3,500 times, these bacteria are stuck to the surface of a tooth in a material called plaque, a mixture of food, saliva and bacteria.

▼ A dental mirror helps a dentist to examine a patient's teeth. Here, the chisel-like incisors can be seen reflected in the mirror. Regular dental checks are important, as they can detect signs of tooth decay caused by a build-up of plaque.

Digestion

The sight, smell or even the thought of food makes our mouth water and stomach rumble. These are signs that the digestive system is preparing for action as a food processor. Most nutrients in everyday food are too big and complex to be used by our bodies. The digestive system breaks down lumps of food into simple molecules, such as glucose, small enough to be absorbed into the bloodstream and carried to where they are needed.

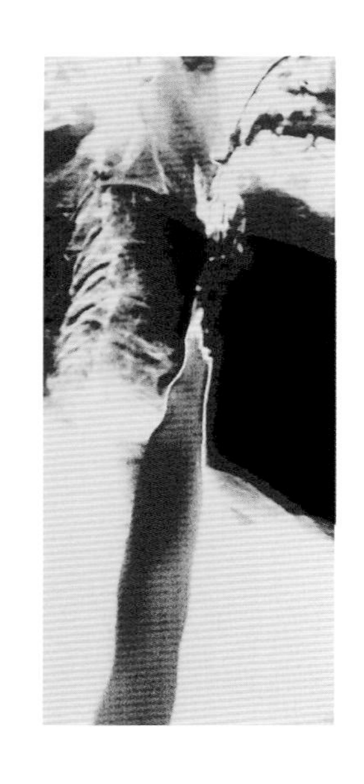

◀ This is an X-ray of the side of the upper body of a person who has just swallowed a barium meal (which shows up on X-rays). In the neck the oesophagus (red tube) has temporarily narrowed. This is caused by muscular contractions called peristalsis.

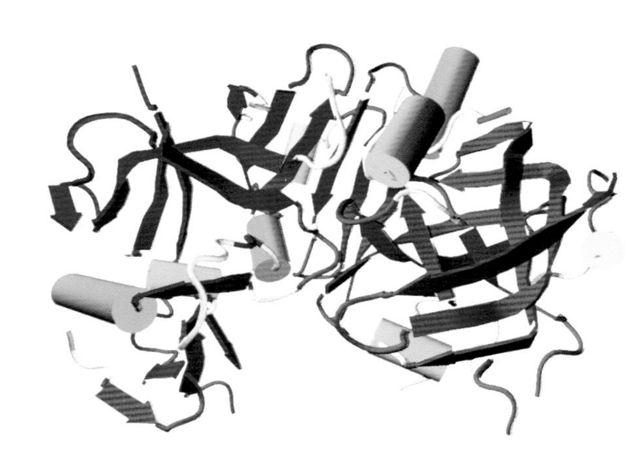

▶ This is a computer model of pepsin, an enzyme that plays an important part in digestion. During digestion, pepsin is released into the stomach, where it accelerates the breakdown of proteins.

Digestion at work

The main part of the digestive system is a long tube called the alimentary canal, which is made up of the mouth, oesophagus, stomach, small intestine and large intestine. The teeth, tongue, salivary glands, pancreas, liver and gall bladder are also linked to the alimentary canal. Two different processes make digestion happen. Mechanical action, such as chewing and stomach churning, physically crushes and grinds food into smaller particles. The action of chemicals called enzymes greatly speeds up the breakdown of food.

Stomach churning

Once chewed in the mouth, food is swallowed and moved by waves of muscular contraction from the throat to the stomach. As food arrives, the J-shaped stomach expands rapidly and the chewed lumps are showered with highly acidic gastric juice. At the same time, the stomach's muscular walls contract to churn and mix food into a part-digested, thickish liquid called chyme. After three to four hours, the pyloric sphincter – the ring of muscle that guards the stomach's exit – relaxes slightly to release squirts of chyme into the duodenum, the first section of the small intestine.

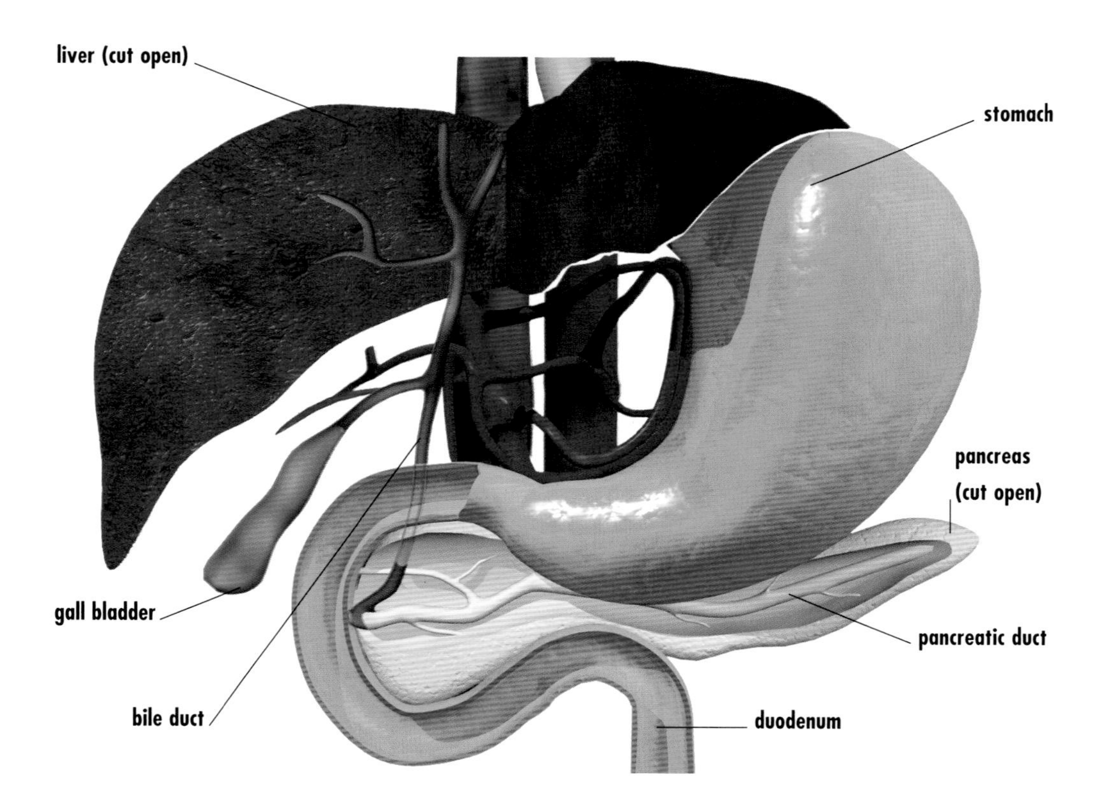

◀ The liver and pancreas play crucial roles in breaking down substances during digestion. Bile from the liver is stored in the gall bladder, then enters the duodenum through the bile duct, while pancreatic juice enters along the pancreatic duct.

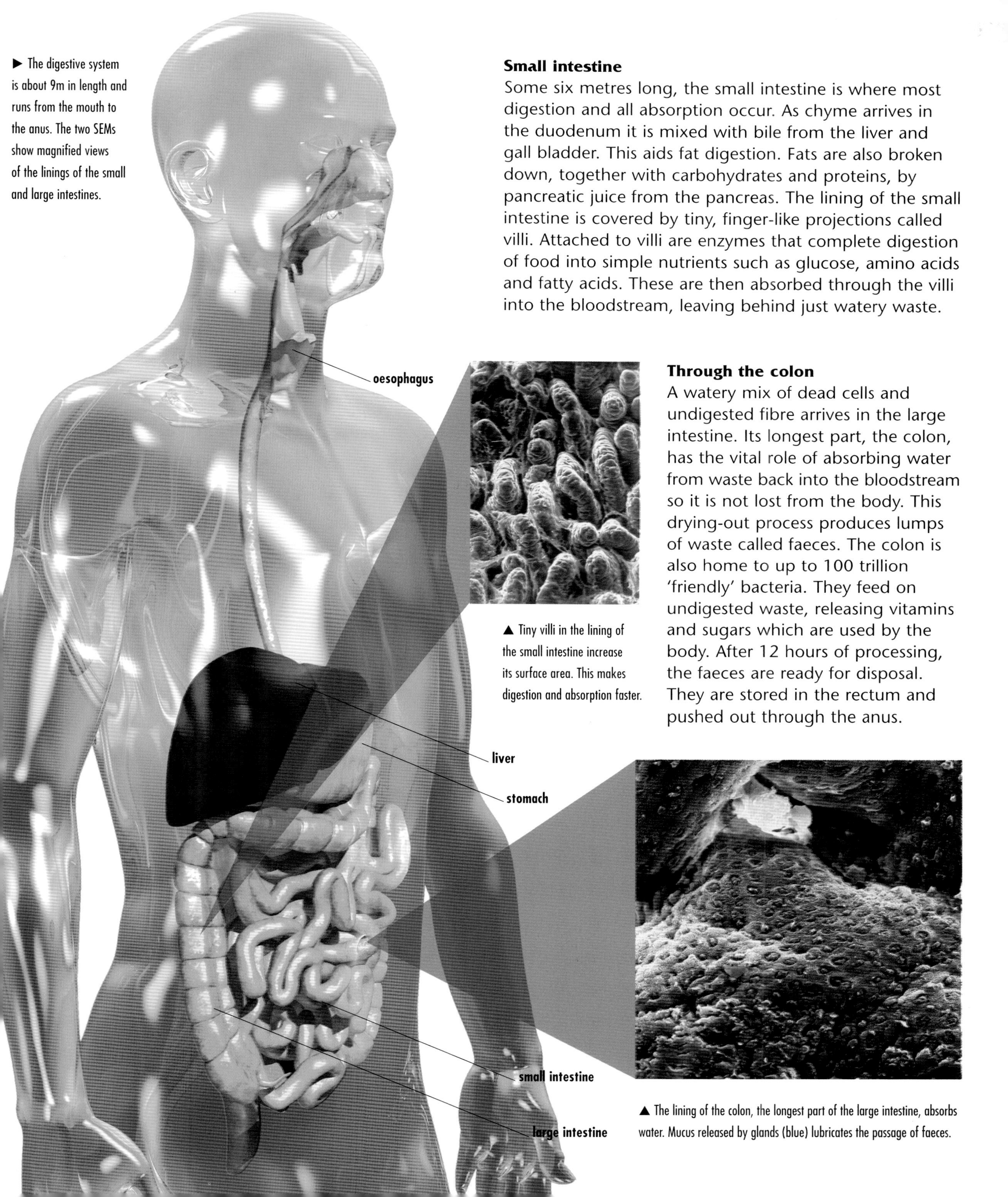

▶ The digestive system is about 9m in length and runs from the mouth to the anus. The two SEMs show magnified views of the linings of the small and large intestines.

Small intestine

Some six metres long, the small intestine is where most digestion and all absorption occur. As chyme arrives in the duodenum it is mixed with bile from the liver and gall bladder. This aids fat digestion. Fats are also broken down, together with carbohydrates and proteins, by pancreatic juice from the pancreas. The lining of the small intestine is covered by tiny, finger-like projections called villi. Attached to villi are enzymes that complete digestion of food into simple nutrients such as glucose, amino acids and fatty acids. These are then absorbed through the villi into the bloodstream, leaving behind just watery waste.

▲ Tiny villi in the lining of the small intestine increase its surface area. This makes digestion and absorption faster.

Through the colon

A watery mix of dead cells and undigested fibre arrives in the large intestine. Its longest part, the colon, has the vital role of absorbing water from waste back into the bloodstream so it is not lost from the body. This drying-out process produces lumps of waste called faeces. The colon is also home to up to 100 trillion 'friendly' bacteria. They feed on undigested waste, releasing vitamins and sugars which are used by the body. After 12 hours of processing, the faeces are ready for disposal. They are stored in the rectum and pushed out through the anus.

▲ The lining of the colon, the longest part of the large intestine, absorbs water. Mucus released by glands (blue) lubricates the passage of faeces.

Waste disposal

Every second, the cells in our body generate waste products and dump them into the bloodstream. All this waste must be excreted, or disposed of, before it builds up, poisons the body and makes us ill. Our lungs, for example, excrete waste carbon dioxide by breathing it out. But the body's main waste disposal units are the kidneys. Daily, they process 1,750 litres of blood, removing excess water as well as waste. The resulting liquid, called urine, is released several times a day when we urinate.

▲ In this illustration from a German medical book of 1517, a doctor examines a flask containing the urine of a pregnant woman.

Making urine

Together with the ureters, bladder and urethra, the two kidneys form the urinary system. Packed into each kidney are about one million tiny filters called nephrons. Fluid is filtered out of the blood into one end of a nephron. As the fluid flows along the nephron, all useful substances, such as glucose, and most of the water are absorbed back into the bloodstream. The water and waste left behind – urine – flows out of the nephron into the centre of the kidney.

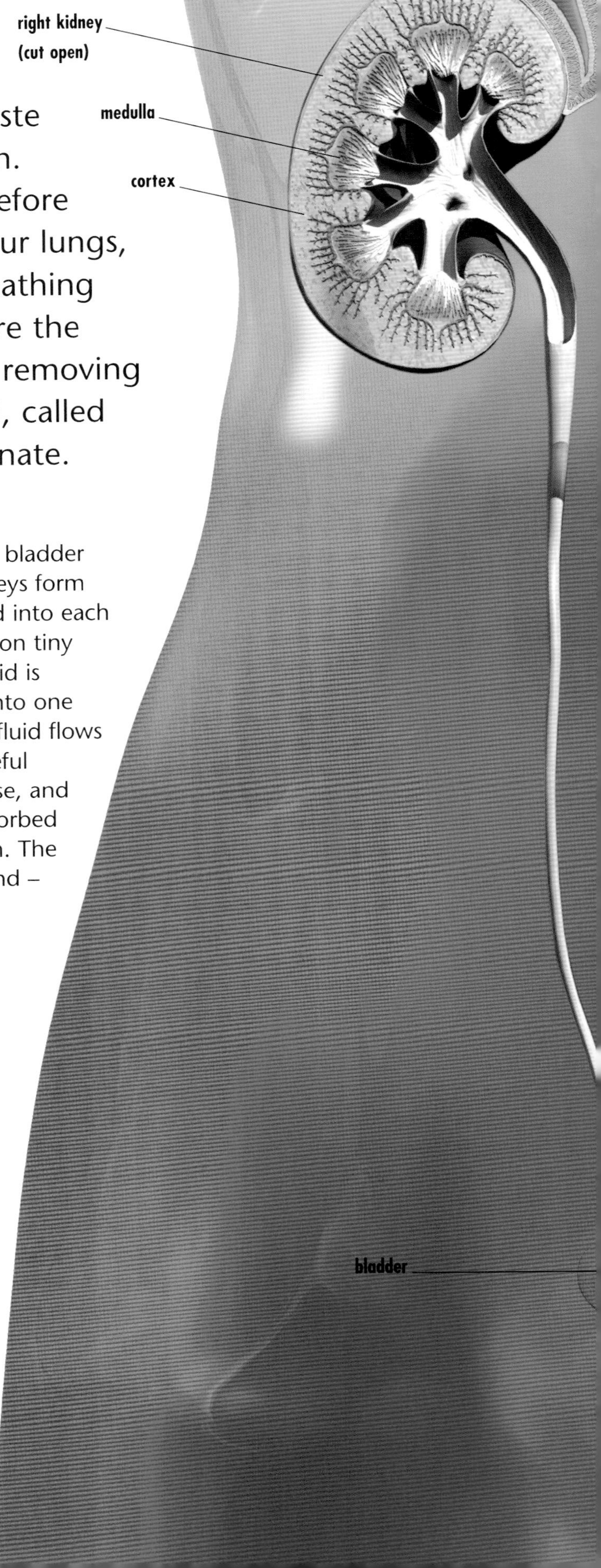

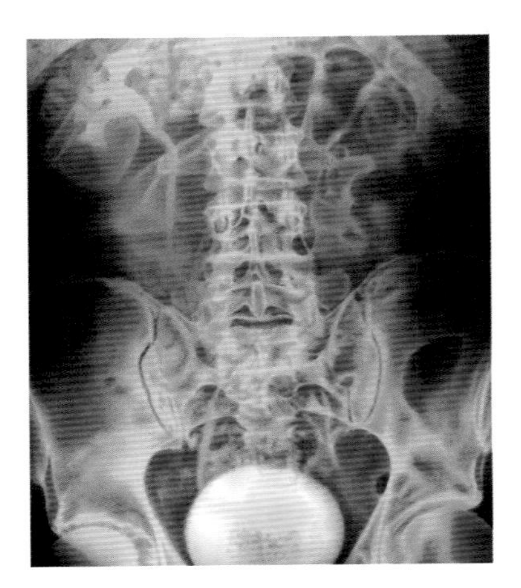

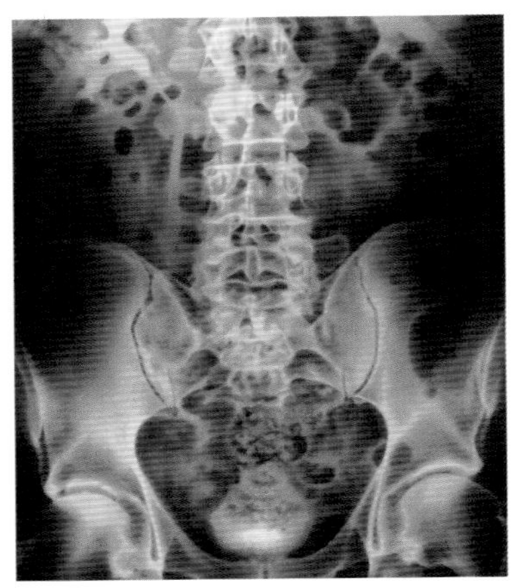

▲ These X-rays, called urograms, use a special dye to show up the bladder. On the left, the bladder has expanded greatly as it fills with urine, while on the right, it has emptied. Rhythmic contractions of smooth muscle in the bladder wall force urine out of the body through the urethra.

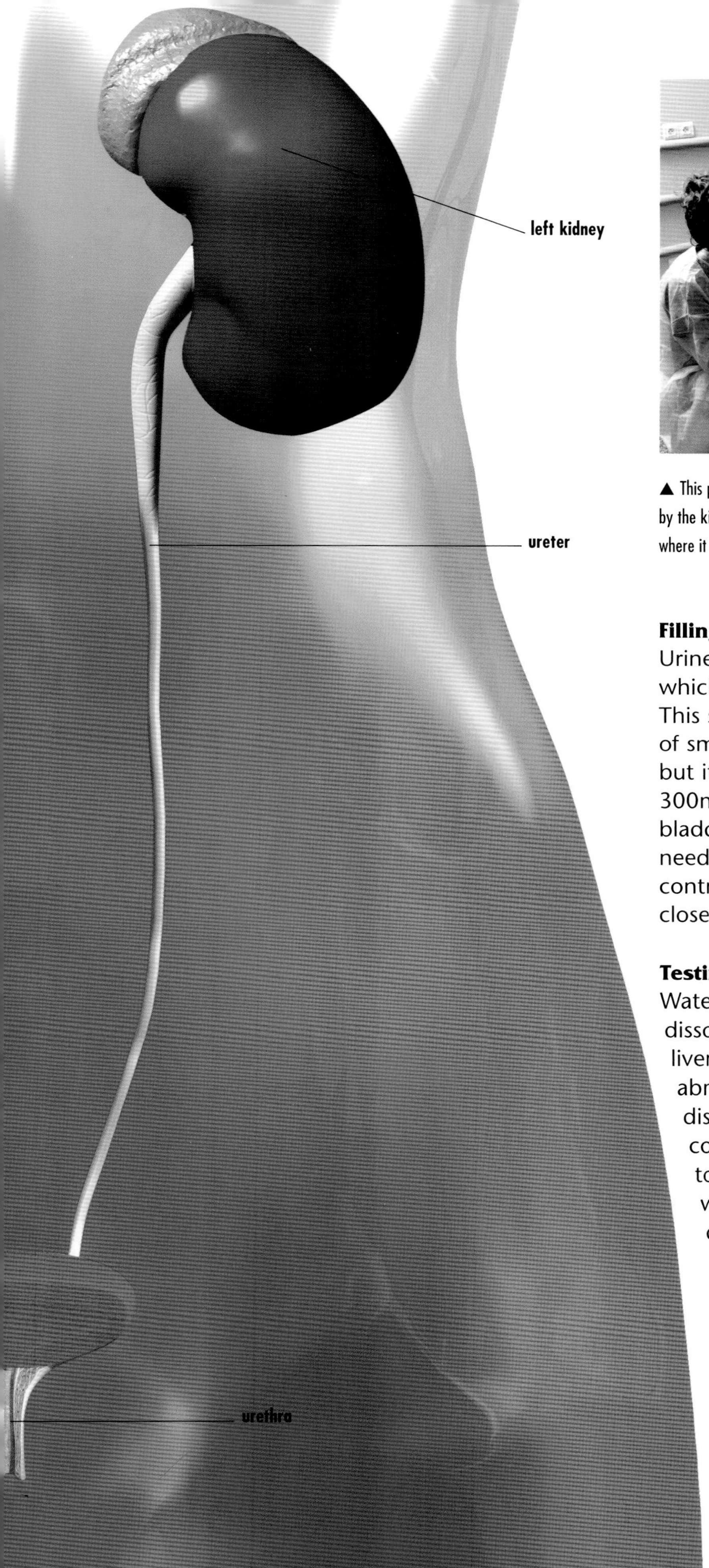

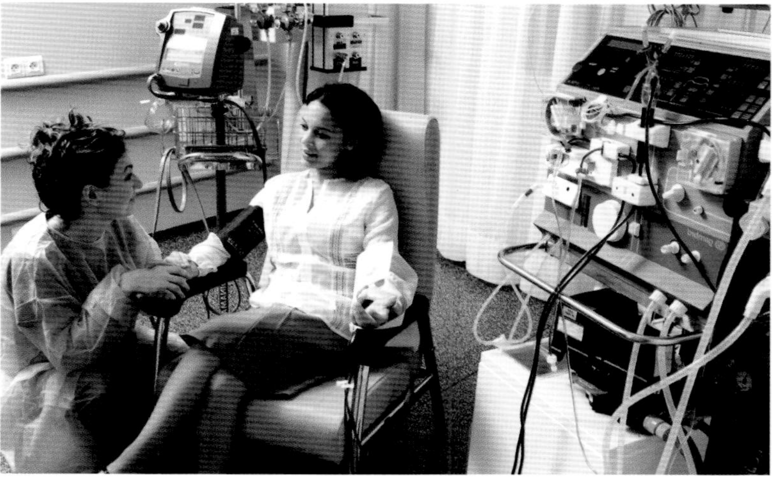

▲ This person's kidneys have failed and no longer work properly. Instead, her blood is cleaned by the kidney dialysis machine to which she is attached. Tubes carry her blood to the machine where it is filtered to remove waste and excess water, before being returned to the patient.

Filling and emptying

Urine trickles out of the kidneys and into the ureters, which have muscular walls to squeeze it into the bladder. This storage bag has a stretchy wall that contains layers of smooth muscle. Empty, the bladder is tomato-sized, but it can expand to the size of a grapefruit. When about 300ml of urine has been collected, messages from the bladder wall are sent to the brain, and a person feels the need to urinate. The urine's exit into the urethra is controlled by a ring of sphincter muscle, which is normally closed. When this muscle is relaxed, urine is released.

Testing urine

Water makes up around 95 per cent of urine, along with dissolved substances, such as urea, a waste made by the liver. Urine is routinely tested by doctors to check for abnormal levels of certain substances that may indicate disease. Before the 20th century, doctors judged the colour, smell and even taste of urine in an attempt to diagnose disease. This technique, called uroscopy, was not very accurate! The water content of urine depends on how much we drink each day. To keep their water content balanced, adults should drink about 1.5 litres of water each day.

◀ The two kidneys are located in the upper part of the abdomen. A ureter links each kidney to the bladder, and a urethra connects the bladder to the outside. The right kidney has been cut open to show its internal workings – the outer part, consisting of the medulla and cortex, contains the filtration units, or nephrons, while the inner part collects the urine they produce. Every day, our kidneys filter 180 litres of fluid from the blood.

Oxygen supply

We breathe air in and out about 20,000 times every day to get enough oxygen – one of the gases in air – to satisfy the demands of the body's cells. Our cells use the oxygen to release life-giving energy from foods in a process called cell respiration. Getting oxygen into the body and removing carbon dioxide, the poisonous waste product of cell respiration, is the job of the lungs and the rest of the respiratory system.

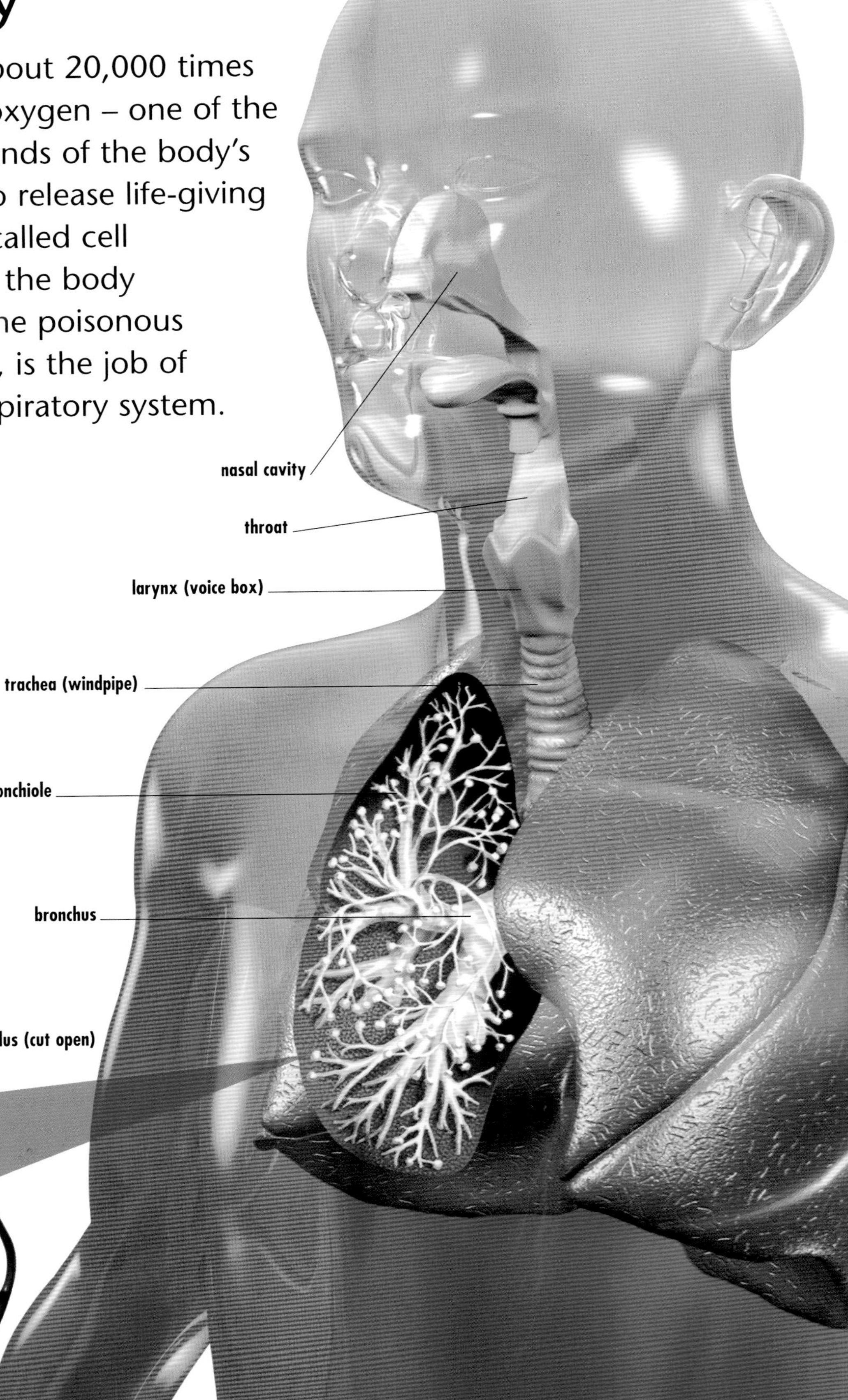

▶ The respiratory system consists of airways that include the throat, larynx and trachea. These bring air into and out of the two lungs. The lungs have a spongy feel and appear pink because of the blood vessels inside.

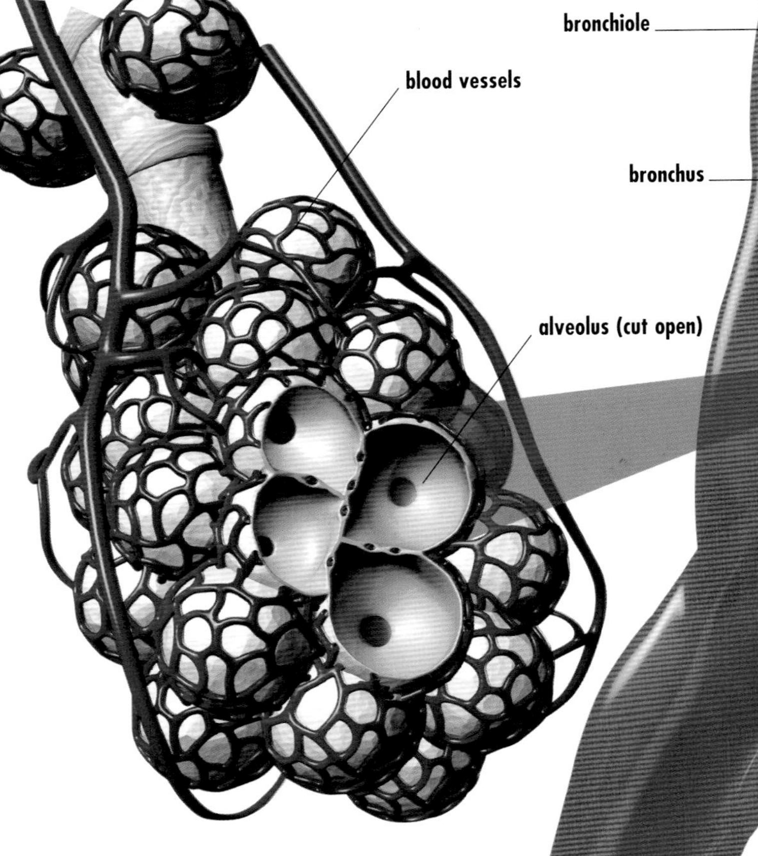

▼ Grape-like alveoli are found at the end of the bronchi. The alveoli are covered in a dense network of blood vessels that carry away oxygen.

Breathing system

The respiratory, or breathing, system consists of the two lungs and the airway that connects them to the outside world. This airway resembles an upside-down tree. Its 'trunk' runs downwards from the nasal cavity through the throat and the larynx, or voice box, and into the trachea, or windpipe. At its lower end, the trachea splits into two 'branches' called bronchi. Each bronchus enters its lung, then divides repeatedly into smaller branches, also called bronchi, and even narrower 'twigs' called bronchioles. The finest of these end in tiny air sacs. There are over 300 million of these sacs, or alveoli, in the lungs.

◄ ▲ Cigarette smoke contains cancer-causing substances called carcinogens that are breathed in by smokers and the people around them. This blackened lung (left) was taken from a lifelong smoker who died from lung cancer as a result of his smoking.

Oxygen in, carbon dioxide out

Oxygen enters and carbon dioxide leaves the bloodstream through the alveoli in a process called gas exchange. As blood flows along the lung's capillaries, oxygen passes from alveoli to the blood, and carbon dioxide passes in the opposite direction. Oxygen-rich blood then leaves the lungs and heads towards the body's cells. Gas exchange is an incredibly efficient process and takes a fraction of a second. Alveoli have a combined surface area of $70m^2$ – that's 35 times greater than the surface area of our skin – packed into a space no bigger than a shopping bag.

alveolus
blood vessel
carbon dioxide
oxygen
cell

◄ During gas exchange, oxygen from air is carried into the bloodstream, and is picked up by red blood cells. Carbon dioxide moves in the opposite direction.

▲ Unlike a fish's gills, human lungs cannot extract enough oxygen from water to keep us alive. But a portable air supply, in the form of an aqualung, means we can explore underwater.

Inhale and exhale

We breathe in, or inhale, and breathe out, or exhale, about 15 times a minute, and more during exercise when the oxygen demands of the body are greater. Our lungs cannot move on their own, but need the help of the surrounding ribs and the diaphragm, a sheet of muscle below them. The movements of the ribs and diaphragm suck fresh air into, and force stale air out of, our lungs. As air is inhaled, sticky mucus and hair-like cilia in the nasal cavity, trachea and bronchi remove dust particles and bacteria.

Heart and blood

In an average lifetime, the human heart beats an incredible 2,500 million times without taking a break. Each heartbeat pumps blood around the body along the blood vessels that reach out to every part of it. As blood flows along these tubes it provides a delivery and removal service to trillions of cells, which require a non-stop supply of nutrients and oxygen, and waste to be removed. It distributes heat generated by the liver and muscles so that our body temperature stays at a warm, steady 37°C. Blood also helps protect the body against invasion by pathogens, or germs.

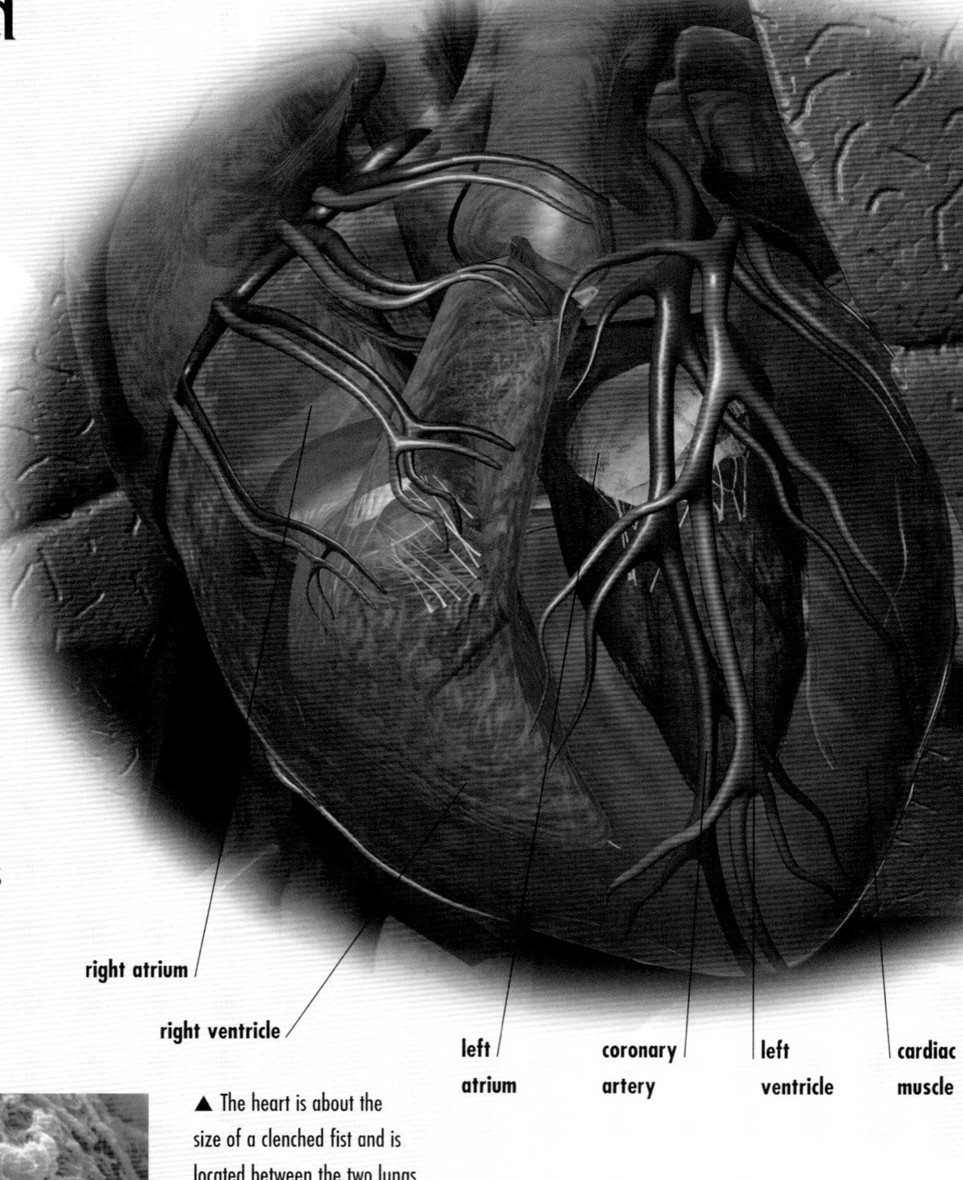

▲ The heart is about the size of a clenched fist and is located between the two lungs. Here you can see its upper and lower chambers – the atria and ventricles – and the thick wall made of cardiac muscle.

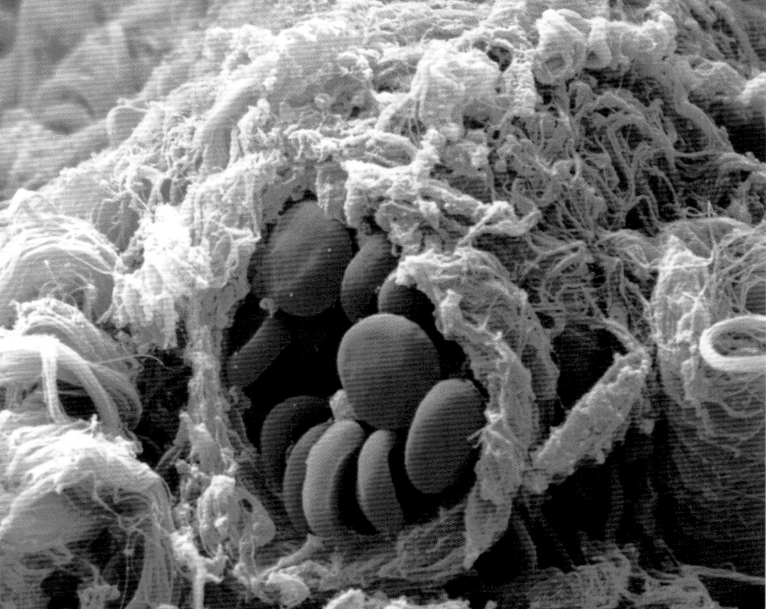

◀ Red blood cells spill out of a very fine blood vessel called a capillary in this SEM. Each blood cell is about 0.008mm in diameter. The walls of capillaries are very narrow – just one cell thick.

Hardworking organ
The heart is a hollow, muscular pump. It has two halves, left and right, each with an upper atrium, and a larger, lower ventricle. During each heartbeat, the right atrium receives oxygen-poor blood, and the right ventricle pumps it to the lungs. At the same time, the left atrium receives oxygen-rich blood and the left ventricle pumps it to the body. The heart is made of cardiac muscle which contracts without tiring and receives its own blood supply through the coronary arteries.

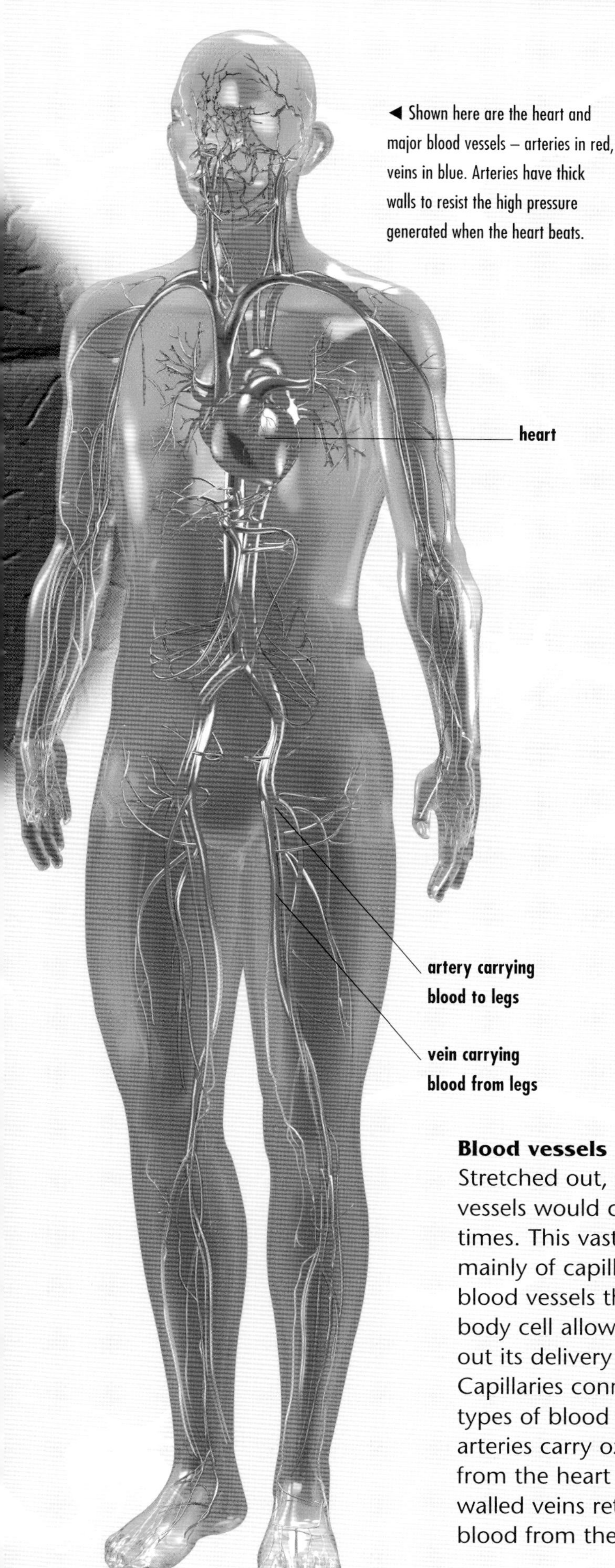

◀ Shown here are the heart and major blood vessels – arteries in red, veins in blue. Arteries have thick walls to resist the high pressure generated when the heart beats.

▲ Magnified 3,000 times, this blood sample shows the three types of cells found in blood. Most numerous are the dimpled red blood cells (red). Rounded white blood cells (yellow), defend the body against pathogens, or germs. Platelets (pink) play a key role in blood clotting.

Living liquid

Blood consists of different types of cells suspended in plasma, a watery liquid that contains nutrients, wastes, hormones and other substances. Plasma makes up just over half of the five litres of blood in an average adult. Red blood cells are packed with an oxygen-carrying substance called haemoglobin that gives the cells and blood its red colour. Red cells carry oxygen from the lungs to cells around the body. White blood cells fight infection by destroying pathogens. Platelets plug openings in blood vessels and help blood to clot, which aids healing.

Blood vessels

Stretched out, one person's blood vessels would circle the earth four times. This vast network consists mainly of capillaries – microscopic blood vessels that pass close to every body cell allowing the blood to carry out its delivery and removal service. Capillaries connect the other two types of blood vessels. Thick-walled arteries carry oxygen-rich blood away from the heart to the tissues. Thinner-walled veins return oxygen-poor blood from the tissues to the heart.

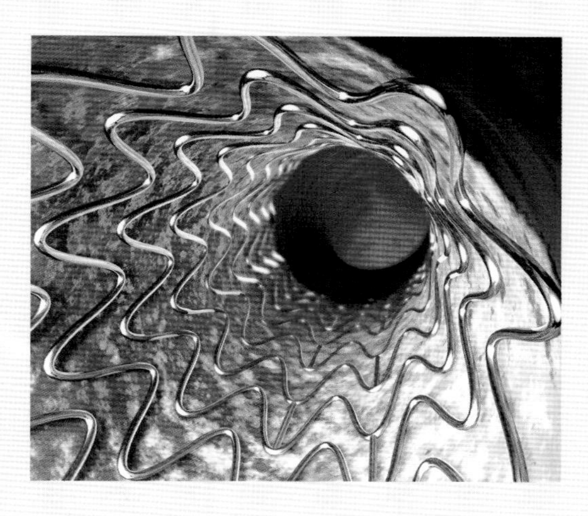

▲ This computer image shows a stent, a device used to hold open and allow normal blood flow along a diseased coronary artery. Heart attacks can result if an artery becomes too narrow.

▲ Tears clear away bacteria and dust as they wash over the eye during blinking. They also contain a bacteria-killing substance called lysozyme.

Defence force

Most of the time, the body machine runs smoothly. Occasionally, however, parts malfunction. Any such breakdown is called a disease. Many diseases, including colds and flu, are caused by tiny organisms called pathogens. Fortunately, the body's defences fight off most invaders. The first line of defence against pathogens are barriers, such as the skin, which physically block the way. Pathogens that get through are pursued by germ-eating white blood cells. At the same time, the immune system, the body's most powerful defence force, swings into action.

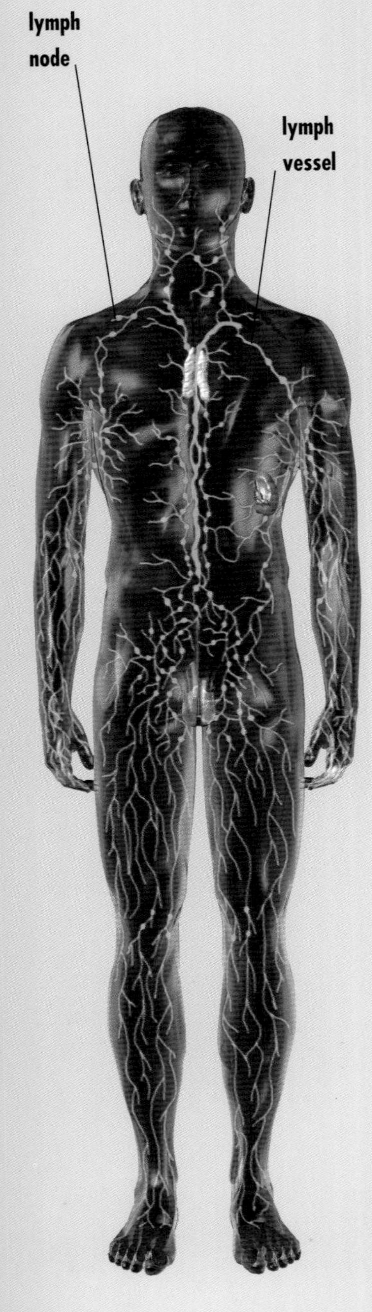

Outer defences

Cells in our skin's epidermis, and those that line the inside of the nose, mouth and throat, are tightly packed together, forming a major barrier against invading pathogens. The respiratory system traps pathogens in sticky mucus, which carries them down into the stomach where they are destroyed by very acidic juice. Pathogens that get through the outer defences are hunted down and eaten by phagocytes. These white blood cells are rushed to the site of an infection through the blood.

macrophage

Immune response

The immune system consists of cells that not only attack but also remember pathogens. Macrophages track down pathogens, while lymphocytes 'remember' specific pathogens and unleash killer chemicals called antibodies. These target and immobilize individual germs and mark them for destruction. If a particular pathogen returns, it is 'remembered' once again and attacked by the immune system.

◀ The vessels of the lymphatic system (coloured green) reach out to all parts of the body. The vessels drain excess fluid, called lymph, from body tissues and return it to the bloodstream by way of swellings called lymph nodes. These contain macrophages and lymphocytes that destroy pathogens.

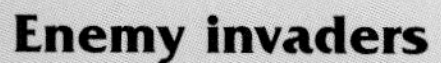

Enemy invaders

The smallest pathogens are viruses, such as the cold virus, which hijack and destroy body cells in order to reproduce. Bacteria – a hundred times bigger than viruses – cause diseases such as whooping cough and food poisoning, and release poisons called toxins. Other pathogens include microscopic fungi, such as the ones that cause athlete's foot, tiny single-celled protists, which cause malaria, and parasitic worms (below). Many pathogens change their 'identity' to avoid the body's immune system, creating new strains of disease that may be even more dangerous.

▲ A nurse looks after a patient during the 1918 influenza pandemic, which killed over 25 million people. Pandemics occur when an infectious disease spreads across wide parts of the world.

microfilaria

▼ Influenza viruses (coloured green) of strain H5N1 usually cause avian (bird) flu. In 1997, it started infecting humans in east Asia and could potentially infect millions of people in the near future.

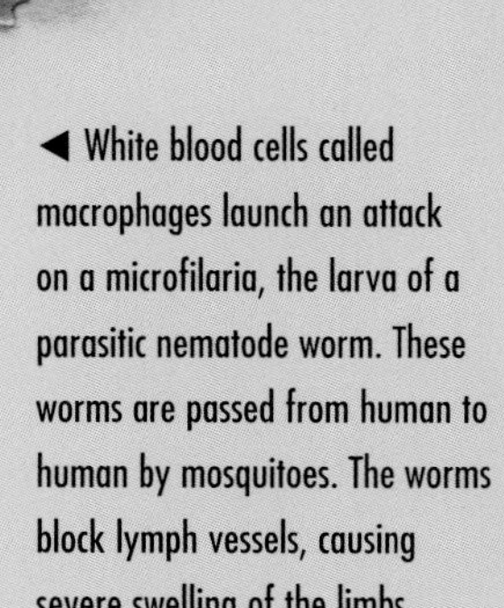

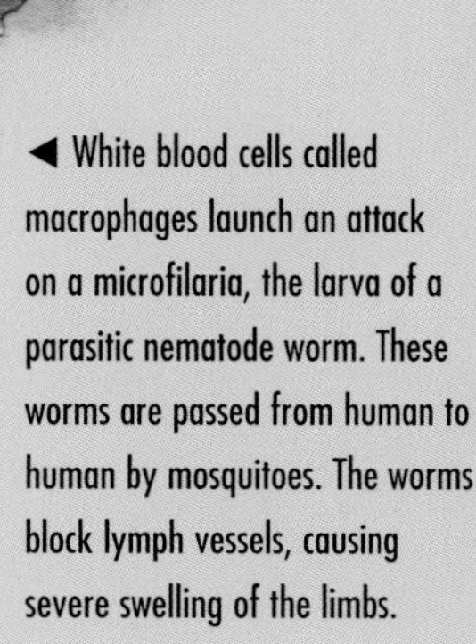

◄ White blood cells called macrophages launch an attack on a microfilaria, the larva of a parasitic nematode worm. These worms are passed from human to human by mosquitoes. The worms block lymph vessels, causing severe swelling of the limbs.

Treating disease

Doctors have many techniques, both old and new, to diagnose and treat disease. Infectious diseases, such as measles or tuberculosis, are passed from person to person, but may be prevented by vaccination or treated with drugs. Other diseases, such as heart disease or lung cancer, are non-infectious. They are triggered by our genes, or by harmful substances in our environment. Treatment of such diseases may involve surgery, drug or other therapy, or even the replacement of body parts.

▲ This capsule endoscope, or 'video pill', contains a tiny video camera, light and transmitter, and is a new tool for diagnosing problems in the digestive system. Once swallowed, it travels along the intestines sending pictures that can be viewed by a doctor.

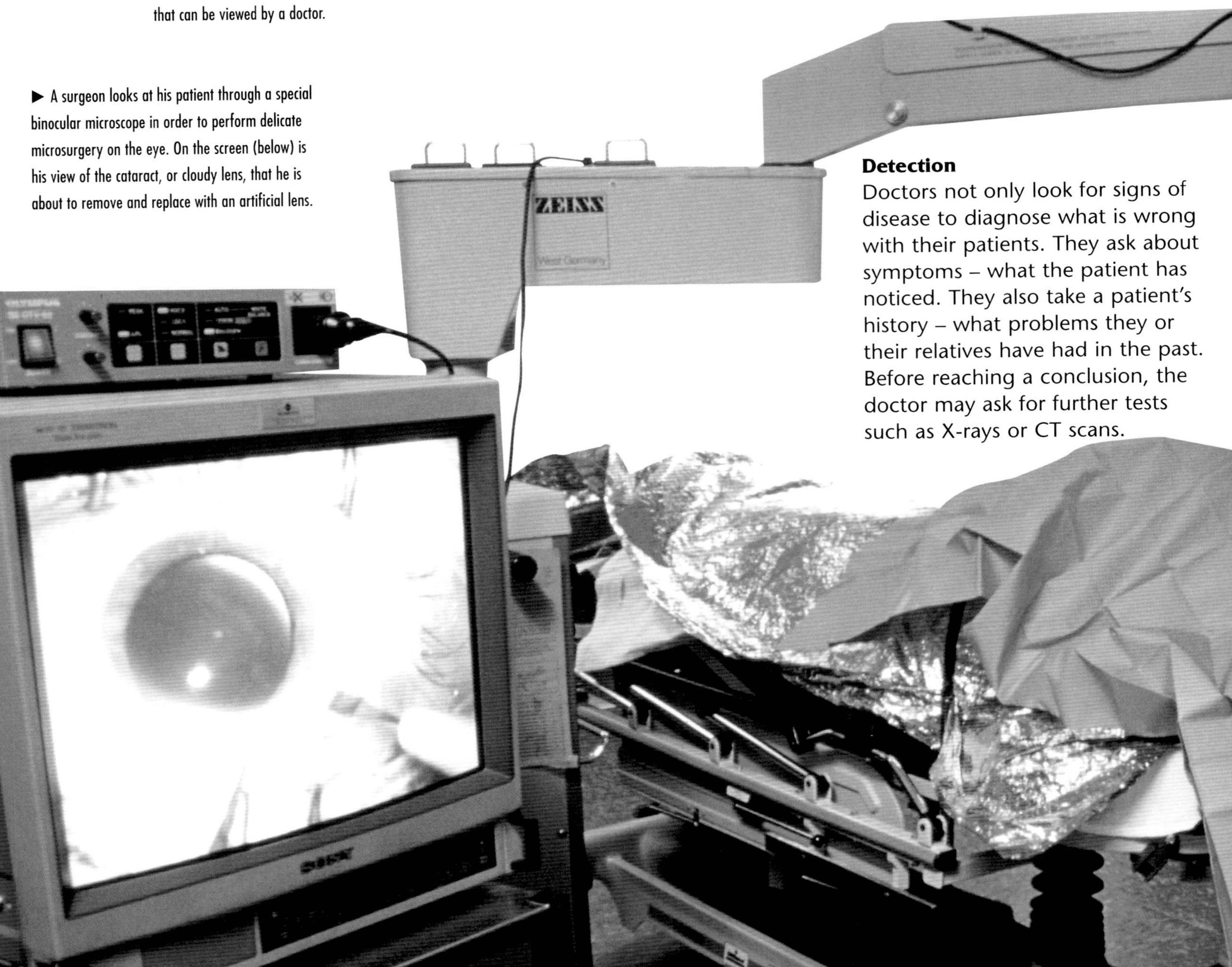

▶ A surgeon looks at his patient through a special binocular microscope in order to perform delicate microsurgery on the eye. On the screen (below) is his view of the cataract, or cloudy lens, that he is about to remove and replace with an artificial lens.

Detection

Doctors not only look for signs of disease to diagnose what is wrong with their patients. They ask about symptoms – what the patient has noticed. They also take a patient's history – what problems they or their relatives have had in the past. Before reaching a conclusion, the doctor may ask for further tests such as X-rays or CT scans.

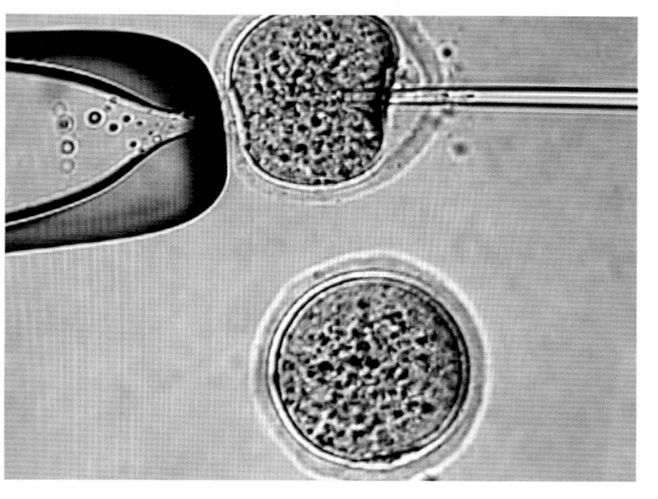

◀ In stem cell therapy, the nucleus, or cell's control centre, is taken from an egg cell and replaced with a nucleus from a body cell. The 'new' cell then divides and provides a source of stem cells. Some scientists believe that these cells could be used, one day, to repair damaged tissues and grow organs.

Treatment
Surgery is one of the wide range of treatments available to treat disease. It involves cutting into the body to remove, repair or replace abnormal or damaged tissues. It takes place in a purpose-built operating theatre, which is kept as clean as possible. Sterile gowns and masks are worn to avoid the spread of infection. Treatment of cancers may require surgery, along with radiotherapy, which uses radiation, or chemotherapy, which uses drugs.

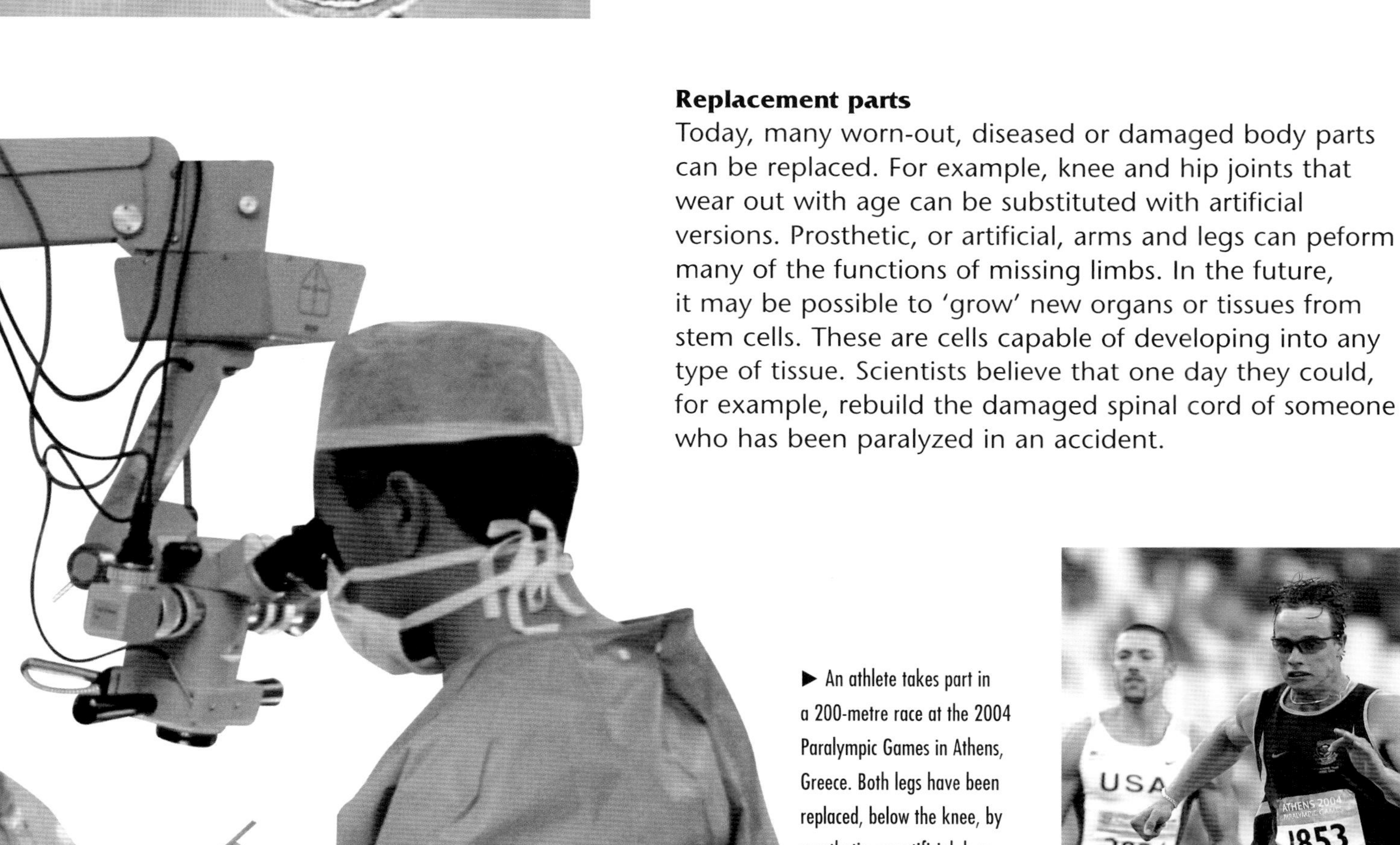

Replacement parts
Today, many worn-out, diseased or damaged body parts can be replaced. For example, knee and hip joints that wear out with age can be substituted with artificial versions. Prosthetic, or artificial, arms and legs can peform many of the functions of missing limbs. In the future, it may be possible to 'grow' new organs or tissues from stem cells. These are cells capable of developing into any type of tissue. Scientists believe that one day they could, for example, rebuild the damaged spinal cord of someone who has been paralyzed in an accident.

▶ An athlete takes part in a 200-metre race at the 2004 Paralympic Games in Athens, Greece. Both legs have been replaced, below the knee, by prosthetic, or artificial, legs. These enable him to run as well as someone with two legs.

SUMMARY OF CHAPTER 3: SUPPLY AND DEFENCE

Feeding the body
Eating food is part of everyday life. It performs the vital role of supplying the body with nutrients. These substances release energy and provide the raw materials for growth and repair. Eating a balanced diet provides the right nutrients in the right amounts. The food that we eat needs to be broken down by digestion before it can be used by the body. Undigested waste is pushed out of the body.

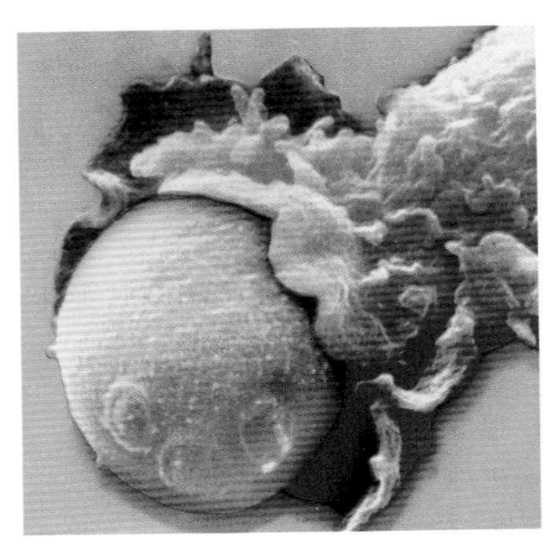

A white blood cell called a lymphocyte destroys a yeast cell by swallowing it.

Waste disposal
The two kidneys dispose of a different kind of waste. Together these organs filter blood, removing the waste products generated by chemicals reactions that take place inside cells. The kidneys also remove excess water. This maintains the body's water content at a constant level. Waste, including urea produced by the liver, together with water are stored in the bladder as urine. This is released through the urethra.

Oxygen and blood
Oxygen, a gas found in the air, is taken into the bloodstream by way of the lungs. Blood cells carry it to body cells where it releases energy from glucose. This process is called respiration. Waste carbon dioxide is returned to the lungs by the blood and breathed out. Pumped by the heart, and carried by blood vessels, blood has other functions as well, including transporting food and hormones, removing waste and distributing heat.

Disease and defence
Blood also contains white blood cells that help defend the body against disease-causing pathogens. Some of these white blood cells make up the immune system which destroys pathogens. The immune system also retains a memory of pathogens so it can launch a rapid attack should they return. Some diseases need surgery, drug therapy or other treatments to cure them.

Go further...

Watch how blood flows through the heart and circulation at:
www.pbs.org/wnet/redgold/journey/circulation_flash.html

See the immune system in action at:
www.learner.org/channel/courses/biology/archive/animations/hires/a_hiv1_h.html

Find out what happens inside the lungs at:
www.mdhs.unimelb.edu.au/bmu/examples/gasxlung

Watch food travel from mouth to stomach at:
www.medical-animations.com/video.php?num=35&type=mov

Cardiologist
Specializes in treating disorders of the heart.

Dietitian
Advises individuals on healthy eating and organizes dietary therapy for recovering patients.

Gastroenterologist
Specializes in the treatment of diseases of the digestive system.

Immunologist
Studies immunity and treats immune system disorders.

Physiologist
Studies the workings of body organs, and how body activities cause internal changes.

Visit *The Giant Heart* at:
Science Centre, Franklin Institute, 222 North 20th Street, Philadelphia, PA 19103, USA
Telephone: +1 214 448 1200
http://sln.fi.edu/giantheart/index.html

Explore the history of medicine at:
The Old Operating Theatre Museum, 9a St. Thomas's Street, London SE1 9RY, UK
Telephone: +44 (0) 20 7188 2679
www.thegarret.org.uk

Learn more about micro-organisms at:
The American Museum of Natural History, Central Park and 79th Street, New York City, NY, USA
Telephone: +1 212 313 7278
www.amnh.org/museum

Glossary

absorption
The process by which nutrients pass through the small intestine into the blood.

atom
A tiny particle of an element, such as carbon, from which all matter is made.

atrium
One of two upper chambers of the heart.

bacteria (singular – bacterium)
A group of simple, single-celled organisms, some of which cause diseases in humans.

cancer
One of a number of diseases caused by body cells dividing out of control.

carbohydrate
One of a group of substances, which includes glucose, that supply the body with energy.

carbon dioxide
The gas released into the air from the lungs as a waste product of cell respiration.

cartilage
The tough, flexible tissue which covers bone ends in joints and helps support the body.

cell
One of the tiny living units from which humans and other living organisms are made.

cell respiration
The process that occurs inside cells which releases energy from glucose.

cerebrum
The largest part of the brain, divided into two hemispheres.

chromosome
One of the 46 thread-like structures composed of DNA that are found inside the nucleus of most human cells.

cilia
Tiny, hair-like structures that are found on the surface of some body cells.

collagen
Tough, fibrous protein that gives strength to tendons and other tissues.

consciousness
An awareness of one's self and one's surroundings.

MRI scan of the head from the side

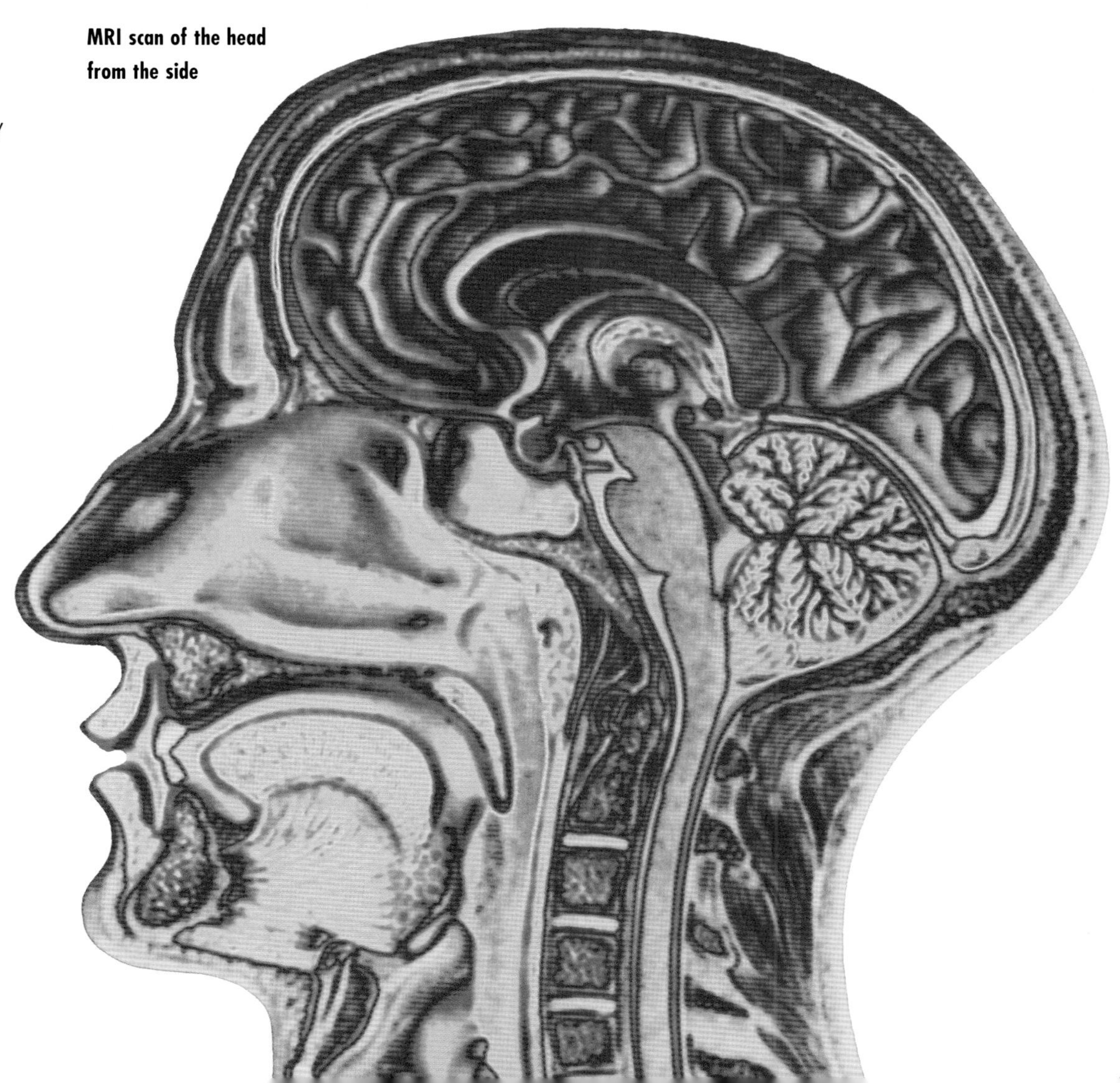

digestion
The breakdown of complex foods into simple nutrients that can be absorbed into the bloodstream.

element
A pure substance, such as iron, made of just one type of atom.

embryo
The name given to an unborn child before the ninth week after fertilization.

enzyme
A type of protein found in the body that greatly speeds up the rate of chemical reactions outside and inside cells.

epidermis
The upper, protective layer of skin.

evolution
The gradual change in living organisms over time.

fertilization
The joining together of the female egg and male sperm to produce a new living organism.

fetus
The name given to an unborn child from the ninth week after fertilization.

fungi (singular – fungus)
A group of organisms, including mushrooms, some of which live on humans.

genome
All of the genes in one of the two sets of chromosomes in a body cell.

gland
A group of cells that release a substance into or onto the body.

glucose
A carbohydrate that provides the body's main source of energy.

immune system
The system, made up of lymphocytes and macrophages, that protects the body from infection by pathogens.

ligament
A tough strip of tissue that holds bones together in joints.

limbic system
An area found deep inside the brain that plays a very important part in emotions and memory.

meiosis
The type of cell division that produces sex cells – sperm and egg – which contain one set of chromosomes.

mineral
One of around 20 key elements, including calcium, iron, sodium and iodine that should be present in a balanced diet.

mitosis
The type of cell division involved in growth and repair that produces two cells identical to the 'parent' cell.

molecule
A chemical unit, such as glucose, made up of two or more atoms.

nerve impulse
An electrical signal transmitted at high speed along a neuron (nerve cell).

nucleus
The control centre of a cell, which contains the chromosomes.

nutrient
A substance in food and drink that the body needs for repair, energy and growth.

organ
A body part, such as the lung or brain, that has a special function or a number of functions.

ossification
The process by which bones are formed.

oxygen
A gas found in the atmosphere that is taken into the body to release energy from glucose during cell respiration.

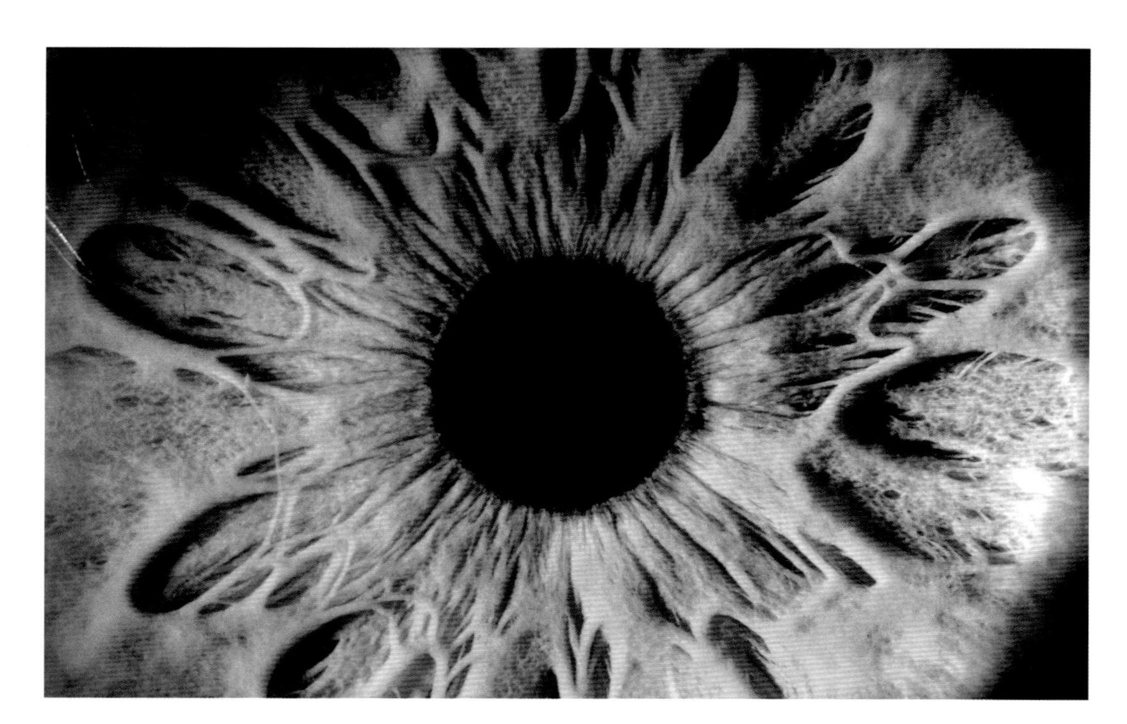

Close-up image of the eye's iris

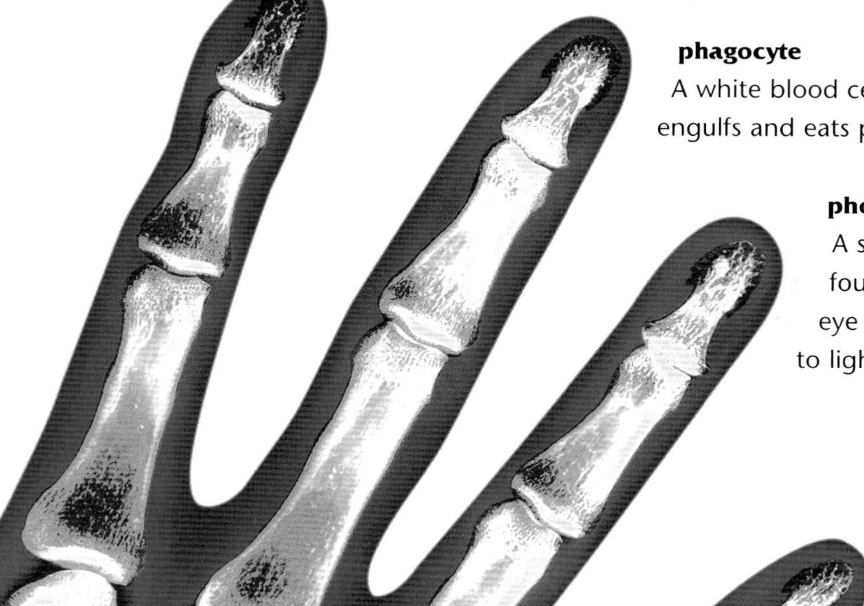

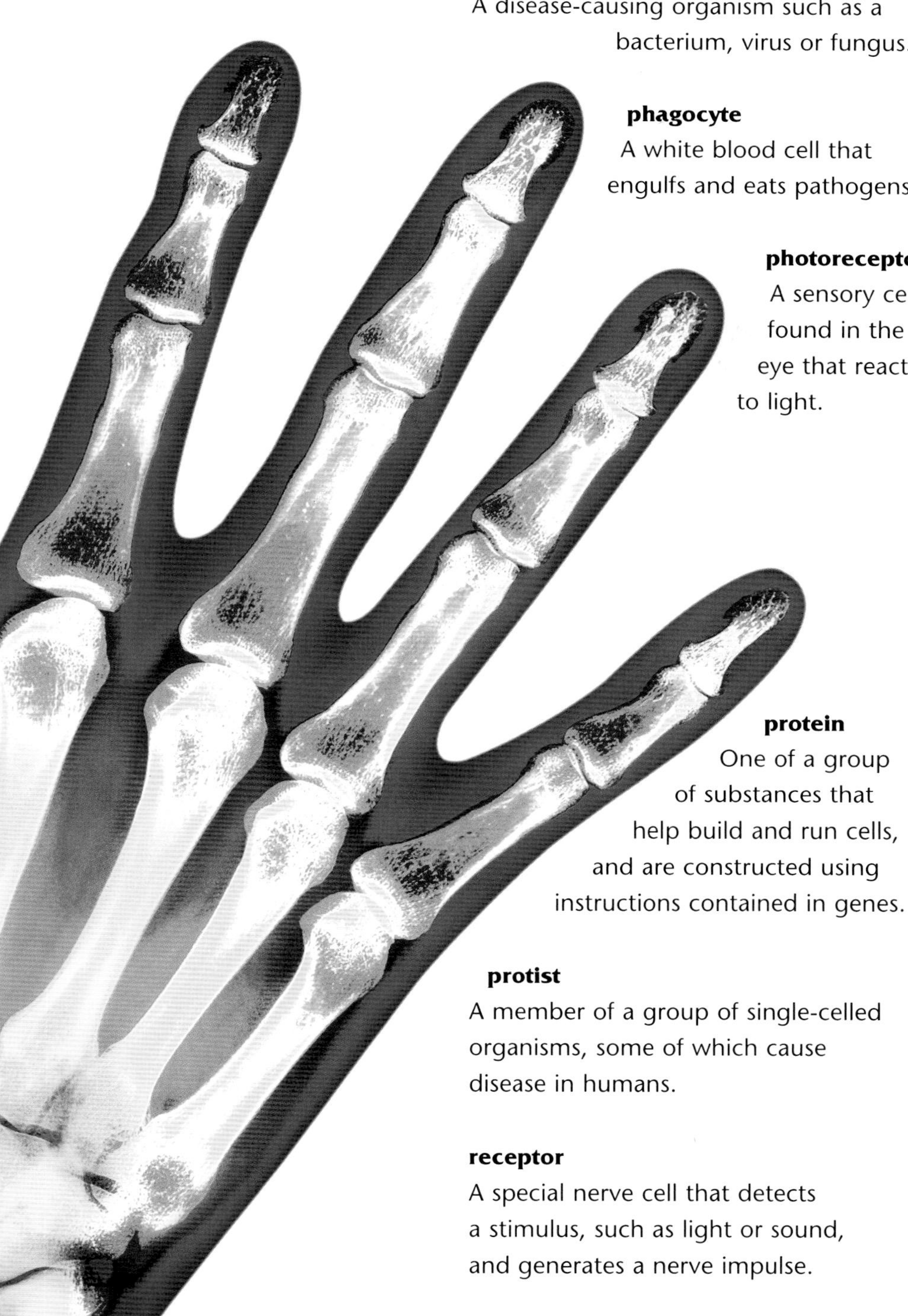

Coloured X-ray of the bones of the hand

papillae
Bumps, which contain taste buds, found on the surface of the tongue.

pathogen
A disease-causing organism such as a bacterium, virus or fungus.

phagocyte
A white blood cell that engulfs and eats pathogens.

photoreceptor
A sensory cell found in the eye that reacts to light.

protein
One of a group of substances that help build and run cells, and are constructed using instructions contained in genes.

protist
A member of a group of single-celled organisms, some of which cause disease in humans.

receptor
A special nerve cell that detects a stimulus, such as light or sound, and generates a nerve impulse.

SEM (scanning electron micrograph)
A photograph produced by a scanning electron microscope that gives a detailed surface view of an object.

SEM of a white blood cell dividing

sex chromosome
One of two chromosomes in each body cell that determine a person's sex.

sphincter
A ring of muscle that controls the flow of fluid from, for example, the stomach.

tissue
A group of the same, or similar, types of cells that co-operate to carry out a particular task.

ultraviolet (UV) rays
A type of radiation found in sunlight that can be harmful to the skin.

urea
A waste substance made by the liver from excess amino acids (the building blocks of proteins).

ventricle
One of the lower chambers of the heart.

vitamin
One of over 13 substances, including vitamin C, essential to a balanced diet.

Index

Acknowledgements

The publisher would like to thank the following for permission to reproduce their material. Every care has been taken to trace copyright holders. However, if there have been unintentional omissions or failure to trace copyright holders, we apologize and will, if informed, endeavour to make corrections in any future edition.

Key: *b* = bottom, *c* = centre, *l* = left, *r* = right, *t* = top

Cover *centre* Science Photo Library (SPL)/Alfred Pasieka; cover *right* SPL/Pasieka; 1*bc* Getty Images/3D Clinic; 2–3 SPL/Mehau Kulyk; 4–5 SPL/Eye of Science; 7*r* The Art Archive; 8*tr* Corbis/Frans Lanting; 8*c* Getty Images/Photonica/David Trood; 9*tr* Corbis/Stephen Hird; 10*tl* Art Archive/Dagli Orti; 10*bl* Art Archive/British Library; 10–11*t* Corbis; 10–11 background Mary Evans Picture Library;11*r* SPL/Mehau Kulyk; 12*cl* SPL/BSIP, Laurent; 12*tr* SPL/CNRI; 12*bc* SPL/Robert Chase; 13 Main image SPL/Geoff Tompkinson; 14c SPL/Dr Tim Evans; 14*tl* SPL/Dr Tim Evans; 14br SPL/Prof. Arnold Brody; 14*tl* SPL/Prof. Arnold Brody; 14*cl* SPL/Eye of Science; 14*bl* Alamy/Phototake Inc.; 14*bl* Getty Images/3D Clinic; 15*cl* SPL/Eye of Science; 15*tr* Alamy/Phototake Inc.; 15*br* Getty Images/3D Clinic; 16*cl* SPL/Anatomical Travelogue; 16*bl* Corbis/Gabe Palmer; 17*l* SPL/Steve Gschmeissner; 17*tr* SPL/Anatomical Travelogue; 17*cr* SPL/BSIP, Jacopin; 18*tl* SPL/Peter Menzel; 18*bl* SPL/Leonard Lessin/FBPA; 18–19*c* SPL/Alfred Pasieka; 19*br* Getty Images/Workbook Stock/Francisco Villarflor Photography; 21*tr* SPL/CNRI; 21*br* SPL/Adrian T Sumner; 22*tl* SPL/D. Philips; 22–23 background SPL/Christian Darkin; 22*br* Phototake/OSF; 23*tl* SPL/Edelmann; 23*tl* SPL/Edelmann; 23*cl* SPL/Corey Meitchik/Custom Medical Stock Photo; 23*bl* SPL/James Stevenson; 23*bl* Mother & Baby Picture Library; 23*br* SPL/Helen Mcardle; 24*cl* SPL/CNRI; 24*c* SPL/CNRI; 24*tr* Getty Images/Brand X Pictures/Elyse Lewin; 25*tr* Corbis/Laureen March; 25*br* Corbis/Tim Pannell; 26*cl* SPL/Pascal Geotgheluck; 27*tc* SPL/Pasieka; 28*tl* Getty Images/Digital Vision/Sun Star; 28–29c Getty Images; 29*tl* SPL/Don Fawcett; 29*br* Getty Images/3D Clinic; 30*tl* SPL/Susan Leavines; 30*cl* SPL/Steve Gschmeissner; 30*bl* SPL/Andrew Syred; 30–31*c* Getty Images/Gary Burchell; 31*br* SPL/Sovereign, ISM; 32*l* Getty Images/Bob Elsdale; 33*tr* Getty Images/3D Clinic; 33*bc* SPL/Alfred Pasieka; 34*bl* Getty Images/Brand X Pictures/Anderson Ross; 35*tl* SPL/AJ Photo; 35*bl* Getty Images/Taxi/Mary Clay; 35*bc* SPL/Arthur Toga/UCLA; 36*tr* Getty Images/Stone/John Rowley; 36*cl* Index Stock/OSF; 37*bl* Alamy/Medical-on-Line; 37*cl* Digital composition by Peter Clayman; 37*r* SPL/Roger Harris; 38*tr* SPL/BSIP, Chassenet; 38*tr*b SPL/BSIP, Chassenet; 38*bl* SPL/Omikron; 39c SPL/Bo Veisland; 40*bl* (combined image) Getty Images/3D Clinic; 40*bl* (combined image) SPL/Anatomical Travelogue; 40*c* SPL/Steve Gschmeissner; 40–41*c* Getty Images/3D Clinic; 40*br* Getty Images/Iconica/ML Harris; 41*tr* SPL/Anatomical Travelogue; 41*br* SPL/Prof. P. Motta/Dept. of Anatomy/University 'La Sapienza', Rome; 42*cl* SPL/Ted Kinsman; 43*t* Phototake/OSF; 44*c* SPL/David Munns; 44–45*c* Getty Images/Taxi/Andreas Kuehn; 45*br* SPL/David Schwarf; 45*br* Getty Images/Stone/Ben Edwards; 46*tr* SPL/Mehau Kulyk; 46*cl* SPL/Dr Tim Evans; 46*bl* Getty Images/3D Clinic; 47*l* Getty Images/3D Clinic; 47*c* Phototake/OSF; 47*br* SPL/Eye of Science; 48*cl* SPL/Jean-Loup Charmet; 47*bl* SPL; 47*bc* SPL; 48–49*c* Getty Images/3D Clinic; 49*tl* Getty Images/3D Clinic; 47*tr* SPL/AJ Photo/Hop Americain; 50*bl* Getty Images/3D Clinic; 50*r* Getty Images/3D Clinic; 51*tr* Corbis/Fabrizio Bensch/Reuters; 51*c* SPL/Matt Meadows, Peter Arnold Inc.; 51*br* SPL/Alexis Rosenfield; 52*bl* SPL/Eye of Science; 52r Getty Images/3D Clinic; 53*l* SPL/Alfred Pasieka; 53*tr* SPL/National Cancer Institute; 53*br* SPL/Hybrid Medical Animation; 54*tl* Getty Images/Paul Dance/Stone; 54*bl* Getty Images/3D Clinic; 54–55*bc* SPL/Eye of Science; 55*tr* SPL/USA Library of Congress; 55*br* SPL/CDC; 56*tl* SPL/James King-Holmes; 56–7*b* SPL/BSIP, Laurent; 57*tl* SPL/James King-Holmes; 57*br* Getty Images/Reportage/Phil Cole; 58*cl* SPL/Biology Media; 59*br* SPL/Alfred Pasieka; 60*bl* Phototake/OSF; 60–61*bc* Corbis/Lester Lefkowitz; 61*tr* Phototake/OSF; 64*bc* Getty Images/Photodisc Red/Zac Macaulay

The publisher would like to thank the following illustrator:
Sebastien Quigley 8–9, 18–19, 28–29, 30–31, 32–33, 34–35, 36–37, 38–39